N A

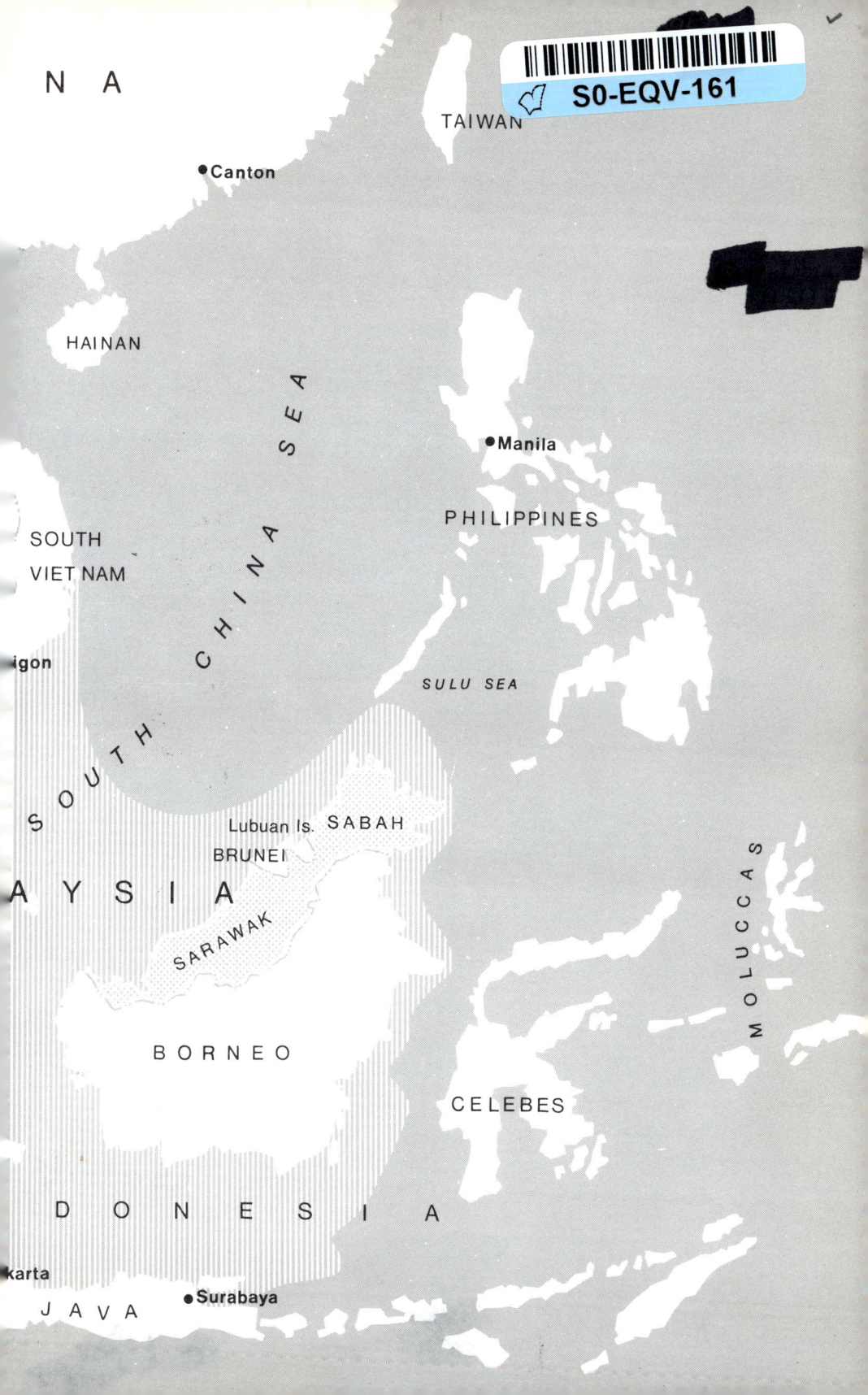

TAIWAN

•Canton

HAINAN

SOUTH
CHINA
SEA

•Manila

PHILIPPINES

SOUTH
VIET NAM

igon

SULU SEA

Lubuan Is. SABAH
BRUNEI

AYSIA

SARAWAK

MOLUCCAS

BORNEO

CELEBES

D O N E S I A

karta
J A V A   •Surabaya

The New Malaysia

East Malaysia
Jesseltor
Lubuan Is.
SABAH
BRUNEI
Niah
SARAWAK
Kuching
BORNEO
0
300
SCALE OF MILES
THAILAND
PERLIS
Alor Star
KEDAH
Kota Bahru
Georgetown
PENANG
KELANTAN
TRENGGANU
PERAK
Taiping
Ipoh
Perak River
Gunong Tahan
West Malaysia
Kuantan
PAHANG
SENGALOR
Petaling Jaya
Kuala Lumpur
Port Swettenham
Klang R.
NEGRI
SEMBILAN
Seremban
MALACCA
Malacca
JOHORE
Johore Bahru
SINGAPORE
Kepulauan Riau
MALAYSIA
0
100
200
300
SCALE OF MILES
Malaysia

The New
Malaysia

I. G. EDMONDS

photographs by the author

THE BOBBS-MERRILL COMPANY, INC.
INDIANAPOLIS   NEW YORK

The Bobbs-Merrill Company, Inc.
Publishers   Indianapolis   New York
Text copyright © 1973 by I. G. Edmonds
Design by Jack Jaget
Maps by Jack H. Fuller
Printed in the United States of America

All rights reserved

ISBN 0-672-51679-9
Library of Congress catalog card number 72-88757
0 9 8 7 6 5 4 3 2 1

To Annette, of course

Contents

	Introduction	ix
CHAPTER ONE	The Land of the Malays	1
TWO	The Rise of Malacca	10
THREE	The City of the Lion	18
FOUR	Life in Early Singapore	30
FIVE	The White Rajah	39
SIX	The Growing Years	48
SEVEN	The Residents of Malaya	59
EIGHT	The Fall of Singapore	70
NINE	Merdeka	83
TEN	Trials of a New Nation	92
ELEVEN	A Nation in Danger	103
TWELVE	The Kuala Lumpur Riots	113
THIRTEEN	Malaysia Today	125
FOURTEEN	Looking to a Troubled Tomorrow	137
	Bibliography	144
	Index	145

Introduction

NO new nation had greater prospects than Malaysia when it was formed in 1963. The nation was created through friendly negotiations and escaped the bloody colonial warfare that has marked the struggle for independence of most new governments. The Malaysian government was stable from the beginning, and popular and able. The country had a favorable trade balance, good economic prospects, and the goodwill of powerful international friends. Under these bright conditions the world expected Malaysia to be a model for other new nations.

But before the new constitution of Malaysia could go into effect, the country was suddenly threatened by greedy neighbors. President Sukarno of Indonesia viewed the formation of Malaysia as a threat to his plans for the aggressive expansion of his nation in Southeast Asia. Then the Philippine Islands demanded the part of Borneo that was to be included in the Malaysian nation. This double-barreled threat was a shock that delayed proclaiming the formation of Malaysia for a time. However, time, diplomacy, British military aid, and a revolt in Indonesia finally settled the trouble among the three nations.

Still Malaysia failed to achieve the potential that her natural resources and political advantages indicated. She next faced a problem and threat that in the long run may prove more dangerous than the greed of her Philippine and Indonesian neighbors. This threat is racism—the pitting of a majority race against a minority race—in a confrontation that has steadily worsened with the years.

In the United States, racial troubles are supposedly the product of skin color. This is not true in Malaysia. There the racial discord is a product of politics and economics. The Malays barely comprise a majority in their country and fear the Chinese, who are the largest minority group in Malaysia. The Malays are afraid the Chinese will seize political power in Malaysia as they have come to dominate the economic sphere of the country. The Malays in turn are determined to "Keep Malaysia for the Malays," as their political slogan proclaims. To this end the Malays framed their constitution to favor themselves at the expense of the minorities. Possession of certain land is restricted to Malays. The bulk of government jobs is reserved for Malay people under the constitution. In every respect government policy is "Malays First." A recent law forces businessmen—mainly Chinese—to hire a Malay quota in middle management positions. These actions of the Malaysia government caused two bloody riots in 1969, and the country faces more racial turmoil in the future as Chinese youth in Malaysia encounter increased frustration.

When Malaysia was formed in 1963 by combining peninsular Malaya with the British North Borneo states and Singapore, the Chinese thought the large number of Chinese in Singapore would give them sufficient pro-Chinese votes to ensure political equality. This hope died when Singapore was expelled from the Malaysian union to prevent Chinese politicians from building up strength.

Older Chinese are willing to accept the situation, but more and more Chinese youth are turning to communism as the answer to their country's racial problem. Such a divided country is fertile ground for Communist expansion. This points to difficult years ahead for the new nation. While both sides realize the danger to Malaysia, the racial problem is not one that can be easily solved in the present Malaysian political climate.

"It is our land—our country. We will not see it stolen from us by the Chinese," the Malays insist.

Introduction   xi

"It is our land, too," Chinese youth reply bitterly. "We were born here and our fathers were born here. We are Malaysians and ask for a 'Malaysia for Malaysians' rather than a 'Malaysia for Malays.'"

The Malaysian government insists that the situation will correct itself and that the problem has been inflated out of proportion by foreign newspapermen. The average Malay and Chinese do not agree. As one put it, "Two races in one country never live in peace. That is true even in your own rich United States where blacks are fighting whites. It is true in the Near East where Jews and Arabs hate each other. And so on throughout the world. 'Never the twain shall meet,' as the Englishman Kipling said."

The roots of the racial problem in Malaysia lie deep in Malay history. Malaysia's written history covers only the last seven hundred years, but accounts coming from other countries indicate that for two thousand years the Malay people have lived under the domination of first one foreign master and then another. Now that they have achieved a national Malay government, the Malays are determined not to permit that government to slip from their control under any circumstances.

This is the story of how this situation came about.*

---

* For purposes of simplification, the name Malaysia refers to the land of the Malays after 1963. The name Malaya refers to the country prior to that time.

The New Malaysia

CHAPTER ONE

The Land of the Malays

THE Malay Peninsula is a narrow stretch of land attached to the body of Southeast Asia. It runs almost a thousand miles due south from the southern borders of Burma and Thailand to separate the Andaman Sea from the South China Sea. Borneo, the Philippine Islands, and the Spice Islands of the Moluccas lie to the east of the peninsula. India is northwest and the rich islands of Sumatra and Java are to the peninsula's south.

The northern two-thirds of the peninsula were claimed by Burma and Thailand centuries ago. The lower one-third, comprising an area of 50,690 square miles, was settled by the Malay people. This area, once called Malaya, is now West Malaysia, which, combined with East Malaysia—the former Borneo states of Sarawak and Sabah—forms present-day Malaysia.

The peninsula's position as a long land barrier across the sea between India and China has made Malaya a key point in Oriental trade routes as far back as history records. The Straits of Malacca (between the southern extremity of the Malay Peninsula and the island of Sumatra) has been a water highway for conquerors, commerce, adventure, and pirates for all the seven hundred years of recorded Malay history. And archaeological finds indicate that trade in this area was carried on by Roman and Phoenician ships before the Christian Era.

The land of the Malays first became important because of its position midway between the rich markets of China and India, and because of its nearness to the Spice Islands of Indonesia. The peninsula lies just north of the equator, and the monsoon winds blow steadily from the northeast for half the year. Then they reverse and blow from the southwest for the remainder of the annual monsoon cycle. This was a tremendous advantage to sailing ships that could sail to Malaya with one wind, pick up cargo and wait for the monsoon change to sail back.

When traders first came to the peninsula, Malaya was almost completely primitive. What few villages there were stood at the mouths of the rivers, and the people lived mostly by hunting and fishing. Except in the alluvial plains, the soil of the peninsula is very poor. This surprises visitors who fly into the country today. From the air the Malay Peninsula is hundreds of miles of unbroken rain forest stretching from the central mountain ranges down to the sea on both sides of the land. Unfortunately, when this jungle is cleared and put under cultivation the soil is rapidly exhausted.

Actually the peninsula is nothing but the tops of mountains that rise out of the sea. If one takes a map of Southeast Asia and draws a line from Burma south along the edge of the Malay Peninsula to Sumatra and Java, and then north around Borneo to the east coast of Vietnam, he will create an outline map of the "Sunda Platform." The platform is an undersea land mass that is sunken to depths of from 120 to 150 feet. The Malay Peninsula is actually a mountain chain rising from this sunken land. The platform creates a shallow sea around the peninsula which geologists consider remarkable for the uniformity of its shallowness.

The mountains that form the Malay Peninsula today were created in the stupendous splitting and folding of the earth which produced the Himalaya Mountains in the Tertiary Era about thirty million years ago. E. H. G. Dobby of the University of Malaysia estimates that the original mountains of the Malay Peninsula were as lofty as the Himalayas but have now been reduced to "stumps of mountains" by millions of years of erosion. This erosion was the direct result of the monsoon winds which later would make Malaya an important trade center. The winds

The Land of the Malays

picked up enormous volumes of water as they blew across the humid equatorial seas. This water was—and still is—dropped in deluging rains on the peninsula. Rainfall averages 80 or more inches a year, but the massive erosion is due as much to the force of the rain as to the water itself.

The huge masses of mud loosened by the torrential rains are carried to the seas by numerous rivers. On the east coast, which fronts on the South China Sea, strong ocean currents disperse this silt. But on the west coast the silt is caught in the fingers of the many-rooted mangrove trees that grow in the water along the shoreline. This captured mud creates huge swamps and is slowly enlarging the land mass at the rate of an inch and a half each year.

None of the peninsular mountains are very high today. Geologists estimate that more than half of their original height has been eroded away by thirty million years of wind and rain. The highest peak today is Gunong Tahan in central Malaysia. Its altitude is 7,186 feet—just enough to get its peak above the mass of the rain forest. On the tip are sparsely scattered scrubs where one can see quartz crystals glittering when the sun is in the right position. Back-country Malays point out this sparkle to visitors as proof that the mountain is one giant diamond. They claim that freebooters through the centuries have often tried to steal the mountain-diamond but were always defeated by sky thunder demons who guard the treasure.

If the listener is skeptical, the old Malay storytellers can prove the existence of these sky demons. It seems that the monsters create thunder during storms by gnashing their huge teeth. Sometimes they do this so violently that their teeth break. They spit the broken pieces out on the earth, where they are occasionally picked up by Malay natives. Scientists claim these "demon teeth" are really Stone Age artifacts left by prehistoric dwellers on the peninsula.

East Malaysia, situated in North Borneo across the South China Sea from peninsular West Malaysia, is even less developed. It is divided into the states of Sarawak and Sabah and is in approximately the same latitude as West Malaysia. The climate is identical and the geography is similar. The settled portions are concentrated along the coast and the rivers. Some aborgine tribes are scattered among the rain forests that are spread across the many hills of the interior. These aborigines, collectively called *Dayaks*, live a nomadic life and are chiefly hunters or fishermen.

Although the recorded history of Malaysia goes back only some seven hundred years, the Malay Peninsula could well be among the oldest inhabited places on the earth. The prehistoric people who first settled present-day Malaysia are believed to have originated in Mongolia. From there they were driven southward by advancing glaciers during the Ice Age. In 1892 bones from one prehistoric creature known as "Java Man" were found in a riverbank in central Java just south of Malaysia. The age of these bones was estimated at about one and a half million years, and anthropologists placed them as being of a species midway between apes and human beings. They do not believe, however, that Java Man (*Pithecanthropus erectus*) is a "missing link" between apes and mankind in the evolutionary chain, but rather that he is a distinct branch. Then in 1927 similar bones (named "Peking Man") were found in North China. These findings seem to indicate that in the Paleolithic (Old Stone Age) period these subhuman creatures migrated down through China and across the natural land bridge of the Malay Peninsula into Java.

No bones similar to Java Man and Peking Man have been found on the peninsula, however. There is evidence that creatures capable of making tools and weapons did live in Malaysia during the last years of the Ice Age. In 1938 a scientist working in the Perak River Valley in Perak Province near the Thailand border found a stratum of gravel whose composition indicated that it had been deposited during the Ice Age. In this gravel was found a number of crude "eolith" tools. Eolith tools, the most primitive artifacts known, are no more than rocks which have been broken and then given a crude cutting edge to be used for chopping. The eolith tools found in the Perak gravel are similar to other Pleistocene artifacts found in India, Burma, and Java.

Just who left these tools is not known, but it does not seem probable that Java Man was sufficiently advanced to have made such tools. The supposition is that they were left by the forerunners of modern man. However, the first clear evidence of human habitation in the peninsula was found in geological

The Land of the Malays

strata of the Mezolithic or Middle Stone Age period. People of this age were cave dwellers. Modern Malaysians, digging bat guano in mountain caves, often find relics of these prehistoric men. The finds have included many human skeletons, animal bones, and Stone Age implements. From these finds scientists have assembled a fairly accurate picture of the Malayan cavemen and their primitive life.

These cave dwellers lived mainly by hunting. Bones found in their caves show that they were not afraid to attack the largest and most ferocious game with their stone-tipped spears. The human bones, however, show that these cave dwellers were not the ancestors of present-day Malays. Malays are small, brown-skinned people of the Mongoloid race who emigrated from China during a long period extending from 1500 B.C. to A.D. 100. The Malays are basically the same type of people who migrated into North Burma, Thailand, the Philippines, Vietnam, and Indonesia. The prehistoric cave dwellers of the Malay Peninsula were apparently closely related to the present-day Melanesians and natives of Papua. Although dark-skinned, they were not related to the Negritos, the small Negroid aborigines who still live in Thailand, the Philippines, and Malaysia.

Thus from about 1500 B.C. there seem to have been three distinct races in the peninsula: the cave dwellers, the Negritos, and the proto-Malays. Apparently the proto-Malays, ancestors of today's Malays, brought in a Neolithic (New Stone Age) culture that in time completely replaced the culture of the Old Stone Age cave dwellers. The tools left by the proto-Malays are comparable to those of the American Indian.

By the beginning of the Christian Era, restless wanderers from other parts of the world began leaving traces of their visits to the Malay Peninsula. One such curious set of relics is a number of beads of Roman and Phoenician design found in Johore state at the tip of the peninsula. These early explorations by ships from the Mediterranean countries sparked an interest in Southeast Asian trade. By the first century A.D., booming trade between India and China increased Malaya's international importance. Ships from India made the 1,200-mile voyage to the west coast of the Malay Peninsula and unloaded their cargo at trade centers. Then ships coming from China picked up the

Batu Caves near Kuala Lumpur are examples of the many limestone caves found in the mountains of Malaysia. Men lived in such caves in prehistoric times. This one has been converted into a Hindu shrine and is of unusual scenic beauty.

merchandise and carried it home. Thus the peninsula originally became internationally important as an entrepôt. In the language of trade, an entrepôt is a port where merchandise is warehoused for transshipment.

Gradually the early Indian traders began doing business with the Malay natives. They swapped Indian cotton for Malay gold, tin, and spices. Although old records call these entrepôt settlements "kingdoms," they were never more than trade villages with a small permanent population to serve the floating crews who came and went with the monsoon winds.

The first settlement in Malaya to become sufficiently important to rate the true name of kingdom was Langkasuka, which was apparently settled by Hindus in the second century A.D. The only historical reference to it is a vague Chinese report that leaves its exact location in doubt. Some historians believe that Langkasuka was located in the present Malay state of Kedah. Others argue that it was farther up the peninsula in what is now Thai territory.

Fragmentary references in old manuscripts mention thirty other "kingdoms" that existed in the peninsula between the fall of Langkasuka and the conquest of the peninsula by Funan in the fifth century A.D. Funan was a Hinduized nation that was founded in Cambodia and South Vietnam about A.D. 100. Funan forced the Malay settlements to pay tribute for almost two hundred years. Then as Funan weakened, it was absorbed by the Khmers of Cambodia. Although the Khmers reached the peak of their power about A.D. 900, they were unable to continue Funan's domination of the Malay states because of the rise of Sri Vijaya, a powerful Sumatran nation on the island of Java just south of the Malay Peninsula. The Sri Vijayan navy established outposts in the Malay states and founded the city of Tumasik on what is present-day Singapore Island. In time ships of the all-powerful Sri Vijayan navy turned pirate and began fighting among themselves. The nation collapsed and was succeeded in power by Madjapahit, another Javanese nation. Madjapahit controlled the Malay Peninsula until the closing years of the fourteenth century.

By this time Madjapahit had grown weak. A group of young nobles, including one named Paramesvara, plotted a revolution.

The revolt failed and Paramesvara fled to Tumasik, which had broken away from Madjapahit and had come under the overlordship of Ayuthia, the kingdom of the Siamese. Here the fugitive Paramesvara staged an attack, slaying the Rajah of Tumasik with the intention of freeing Tumasik from Siamese control. Paramesvara overestimated his ability to fight the vengeful Siamese and had to flee with his closest followers. They finally settled at the trading post of Malacca about 75 miles up the west coast from Tumasik.

Although not a large place, Malacca was important because a road had been hacked through the jungles from Malacca to the east coast of the peninsula. Cargo could now be unloaded at Malacca, transported overland a hundred miles, and reloaded onto Chinese ships on the east coast. This route eliminated the slow sail through the Straits of Malacca, around the tip of the peninsula and through the South China Sea.

At first Paramesvara kept in hiding. Then the arrival in Malacca of a Chinese naval expedition gave him a chance to defy the Siamese. The expedition was under the command of a famous admiral by the name of Cheng Ho who had been dispatched by the Ming Emperor of China to add new territory to the empire. China, under the Mings, was not interested in occupying territory beyond the Chinese mainland, but did want neighboring countries to acknowledge Chinese suzerainty. This served a double purpose. It prevented the buildup of powerful neighbors on China's frontiers who might someday threaten the empire, and it permitted the Ming Emperor in Peking to feel that he was master of the entire world. In return for acknowledgment of Chinese overlordship, the Ming dynasty emperors never interfered in the internal operations of their subject countries as long as an annual tribute was paid to Peking. This tribute was small and never burdensome. The subject countries looked upon it as insurance against attacks by their own enemies.

Paramesvara welcomed Cheng Ho. Both men were Muslims, and this got their friendship off on a firm religious foundation. The religion of Islam, introduced into the Malay states by Indian Muslims and Arab traders, spread with such rapidity that it eventually became the predominant religion in the Malay Peninsula. Paramesvara lavishly entertained the Chinese visitors and readily acknowledged China's suzerainty over Malacca. He personally delivered the first tribute payment to Peking. After this, any attack on Malacca by the Siamese King would be interpreted by the Ming Emperor as an attack upon himself. Now safe behind the shield of China's might, Paramesvara set out to make his city-state the most powerful on the peninsula.

CHAPTER TWO

The Rise of Malacca

PARAMESVARA'S founding of a sultanate in Malacca in 1409 coincided with the demand in Europe for spices from the Orient. Lack of refrigeration caused meats to spoil quickly and spices were needed to disguise the putrid taste. By this time the art of shipbuilding had improved to the point where vessels could carry sufficient sails to make long voyages. European ships sailed around India, where they picked up spices that Indian traders brought from the Malay entrepôts which in turn were supplied by local ships sailing between Malaya and the Spice Islands.

Malacca was in an excellent position to take advantage of this booming trade. In a short time the Malaccan harbor became a maritime melting pot, jammed with lateen-sailed *dhows* from Arabia, junks from China, *praus* from neighboring islands and dugout canoes from upriver in the Malayan highlands. In time this motley collection would be joined by galleys from Venice, caravels from Spain, and cargo vessels from Portugal.

In 1414 Paramesvara made additional trips to Peking to ensure Chinese aid against the growing Siamese threat. When Paramesvara died in 1428 he was succeeded by his son Sri who renounced the Muslim religion, but this did not affect his subjects, who kept converting to Islam in large numbers. At this time Siam became convinced that China had lost interest in Malaya and sent an army mounted on war elephants down the peninsula

The Rise of Malacca

to crush Malacca. Just when it seemed that the city-state was lost, Cheng Ho, the Chinese admiral, suddenly sailed into Malacca harbor. The Siamese hastily withdrew.

In the years that followed, Malacca grew in importance as a world trade center but faced grave internal problems. The first was a power struggle that followed Sri's death in 1444. At this time angry Muslims refused to serve any longer under a Hindu ruler. They murdered Sri's son, Deva Shah, causing a civil war between Hindus and Muslims. The Siamese to the north took advantage of the civil strife to try to take over Malacca. The Malay hero whose military genius saved Malacca this time was named Tun Perak.

The fighting ended, leaving Tun Perak as Malacca's strong man, a position he maintained for the next forty-two years. From 1456 to 1498 he was the real ruler of Malacca, although he never took the throne himself. He was content to be a king-maker and to rule through puppets he placed on the throne. During these years Tun Perak teamed up with another Malay hero, Hang Tuah. Tun Perak developed basic strategy and handled political affairs while Hang Tuah led the Malaccan army in a series of conquests that brought all the southern part of the peninsula under Malaccan control.

Trade continued to grow, aided by Tun Perak's free trade policy. The sultans of Java, Sumatra, and the Molucca Islands put heavy customs taxes on trade in their ports. Religious fanatics controlling some of the other ports imposed extremely stringent religious and racial restrictions on trade. On the other hand, under Tun Perak everyone was welcome in Malacca's port, which soon became the most important trade center between China and India.

The fifty years from 1446 to 1496 are considered the Golden Age of Malaya. Thousands of vivid stories have come down about the heroes and mighty deeds of this time. Unfortunately, most of them are either legendary or so embroidered with fiction that they are scarcely credible. The *Malay Annals,* an old collection of stories, is the chief written source of the Malaccan period. It is not a chronological account and much of it can be dismissed as legend. However, the tales are often fascinating and do throw light on the life of the times.

Although the shrewd Tun Perak was *bendahara*—prime minister—and the power behind the throne, occasionally one of his puppets showed some spirit. One of these was Ala'uddin, who occupied the Malaccan throne from 1477 to 1488. The *Annals* tell how he restored law and order to the city. It seems that Tun Perak believed in providing for his relatives. He appointed a nephew to the position of *temenggong,* chief of the national police.

As a port jammed with every nationality in the East, Malacca naturally had a high rate of crime. The situation became so bad that Sultan Ala'uddin became concerned. Like the legendary Haroun al-Raschid of the *Arabian Nights* in Bagdad, Ala'uddin disguised himself and went out at night to observe conditions at firsthand. On one of these nightly expeditions the sultan saw five thieves making off with a chest of money. Ala'uddin and his two companions attacked the thieves, killing two of them and putting the others to flight. The sultan then cautioned his companions to say nothing of the adventure until he should tell them to do so.

The next morning the sultan told the temenggong that there had been two deaths and a robbery the previous night. The official pleaded that he could do nothing since there were so many criminals. Ala'uddin then had the stolen chest brought in while one of his companions explained how the two thieves had died. The sultan then pointedly told the temenggong: "Perhaps I should take over your position, for I seem to be able to do a better job of policing!" The *Annals* went on to say that the temenggong, despite his secure position as Tun Perak's nephew, got the message and did a better job of keeping order in Malacca.

However, Ala'uddin did not always get his way. Soon after Ala'uddin was made sultan by Tun Perak, Ala'uddin's older brother, angry at being passed over for the throne, seized Pahang state in central Malaya and demanded that the coastal states pay tribute to him instead of to Ala'uddin in Malacca. Ala'uddin wanted to make war against his rebel brother, but was restrained by Tun Perak who brought about a reconciliation between the two brothers.

Ala'uddin died in 1488, giving Tun Perak the opportunity to appoint his fourth sultan. The old prime minister selected his grandnephew, a child named Mahmud Shah. By this time Tun Perak was so old that he had no interest in anything except maintaining things as they were. As a result, Malacca's power started to decline. In those days of ceaseless conquest a nation that lost its aggressiveness was on the road to disaster. Tun Perak's fifty-year-long domination of Malacca finally came to an end in 1498, when he died. He was succeeded by his brother, Tun Puteh, who lived for only another two years. The position of prime minister passed to Tun Mutahir, the temenggong who had been rebuked by Ala'uddin years before. Mutahir had not improved much, but the weak sultan, Mahmud Shah, could do nothing about Mutahir's cruelty and corruption which were undermining the government.

Then in 1509, nine years after Mutahir came to power, a Portuguese vessel arrived in Malacca. The Portuguese asked for trading privileges. Mutahir, in a reversal of Malaccan free trade traditions, refused to see the foreigners and sent troops to seize the Portuguese ship.

According to John Cameron, who wrote an engaging (but not always accurate) history of early Malaya: "De Sequeira, the Portuguese captain, turned his cannon on the Malay enemy. The effect was thus described in the *Malay Annals:* 'All the people of Malacca were frightened when they heard the sound of cannon; saying, what sound is this thunder? And the bullets came and struck the people on the land, and some had their necks severed, and some had their waists, and some their hands and feet, and they said what is the name of this weapon, which is so round; it is not sharp, yet will it kill.' "

The weapon that so awed the Malaccans was a 12-pounder— a cannon that shot a 12-pound iron ball. While it is true that the Portuguese were the first Europeans to reach the Orient, it seems incredible that the Malaccans had never seen cannon before.

In any event, this was the beginning of the end for free Malacca. Communications were slow in those days, and it was three years before the Portuguese viceroy of Goa, Alfonso d'Albuquerque, was able to send a navy to teach the Malaccans respect for ships from Portugal.

Portugal was then at the height of her glory. Her daring sailors were ahead of the rest of Europe in exploring and establishing trade with the Orient. However, the Portuguese were not interested in colonization or in the acquisition of great expanses of empire, as were the Dutch and British who followed them. The Portuguese only wanted sufficient land to establish trading centers and entrepôts. In India they took only Goa, a small city-state on the west coast, which became their Asian headquarters. Similarly, d'Albuquerque wanted only the port of Malacca which he could use as a Malay Peninsula base.

When d'Albuquerque arrived off Malacca in August 1511, Mutahir, who made the attack on De Sequeira's ships, was dead. He was killed while trying to overthrow Sultan Mahmud Shah. D'Albuquerque delivered Mahmud an ultimatum, demanding the surrender of the city. When the sultan refused, the Portuguese bombarded the port. Mahmud tried to rally his people, but the Malays were the only ones who would fight. The Chinese and Indian traders in Malacca refused to help, for their businesses had been badly hurt by Mutahir's greed and they welcomed the Portuguese attack. Mahmud and his Malays fought valiantly, but their *krises* (daggers) and swords were no match against d'Albuquerque's cannon. The city fell in August 1511, after a week's fighting.

Mahmud had been a poor ruler up to this time, but the loss of his capital city put steel into him. He retreated to Johore state on the tip of the peninsula where he began to rebuild his shattered army. In the years that followed he made numerous attacks on Malacca but never was able to retake the city. After his death the Malaccan sultanate he represented gradually weakened and was overthrown by a new Johore sultanate which continued to battle the Portuguese. At one point the vengeful Malays reduced the Portuguese defenders of Malacca to only thirty men. They would have retaken the city if help from Goa had not arrived in time to prevent a Malay victory.

The Portuguese, realizing that they could not always depend on aid coming from Goa at a providential moment, built a tremendous stone fort that was the marvel of its day. Commentators have made much of the fact that the fort had no sally ports through which the defenders could launch counterattacks against a besieging enemy. Actually this was by design. The Portuguese never kept a large force of soldiers in Malacca.

Malaccan-Portuguese trade, while sufficient to maintain the port, was never as large as it had been under Tun Perak's free trade policy. Native traders found that the Portuguese treated them even worse than Mutahir had done, causing many to move their businesses to ports in Java and Sumatra. Under these depressed conditions, the Portuguese could not afford to garrison a large number of soldiers in Malacca. The extremely strong fort was intended to make up for the small number of troops.

By 1541 a new power, the sultanate of Acheh, had grown up on the island of Sumatra and soon clashed with the Portuguese over rights to the Sumatran pepper trade. This began a three-way fight among Malacca, Acheh, and the Johore Malays. As the fighting went on, Acheh encroached more and more upon Malay territory in Johore. This forced Johore to make a truce with the Portuguese in Malacca, with whom they joined forces to resist Acheh aggression. The temporary allies gave Acheh such a beating in 1582 that Johore felt safe in breaking the alliance with the Portuguese and resuming her attempts to retake Malacca. The Portuguese successfully defended their stolen city and retaliated by sacking Johore Bahru, the Johore state capital, in 1587. Fighting continued for the rest of the century.

As the sixteenth century drew to a close, a far more formidable European enemy than the Portuguese began moving into Southeast Asia. This enemy was the Dutch. For two hundred years the Netherlands had been part of the Holy Roman Empire, but in the last days of the empire the Dutch had been practically autonomous. Then early in the sixteenth century, dismemberment of the Holy Roman Empire gave the Netherlands to Spain. Philip II of Spain sent the dreaded Spanish Inquisition to the Netherlands with orders to stamp out Protestant heresy and to force the Dutch to accept Spanish Catholicism.

The Dutch revolted, starting a war for independence that lasted eighty years. During this long struggle, a large part of the cost of the war was met by profits made by Dutch merchant vessels that bought Asian spices in Portugal and resold them in Europe. This profitable arrangement with the Portuguese ended abruptly in 1580 when Philip II of Spain gained control of Portugal. The loss of the spice trade was a serious blow to the Dutch economy, but in 1588 Sir Francis Drake and his English naval forces smashed the Spanish Armada, weakening Spain so badly that fighting practically ceased between Spain and the Netherlands, although the war continued officially until 1640.

When Philip II closed Portugal's ports to the Dutch he forced the Netherlands to go directly to Southeast Asia for their spice cargos. Since Portugal was now part of Spain, the Netherlands' old enemy, Dutch captains had no qualms about attacking Portuguese outposts in the Orient. By 1633 the Dutch were sufficiently strong to blockade Malacca but were not able immediately to reduce the famous fort there. The fighting went on for seven years before the fort fell because Portugal was unable to send reinforcements.

Malacca was never very important under Dutch rule, although the new rulers tried hard to revive the port's former glory as the greatest trade center in Southeast Asia. The trouble was that Malacca's former success was based on Tun Perak's free trade policy while the Dutch founded their operations on monopolies. They worked to gain exclusive trading privileges in their territories and vigorously excluded all ships not belonging to the Dutch East India Company—or else they tried to collect exorbitant tariffs and custom fees from the foreign traders. The Dutch were also hampered by the rising might of the Bugis people from Celebes, a curiously shaped island beyond Borneo. These warlike people were determined to conquer the Malay Peninsula.

European historians have written glowingly of Portuguese and Dutch activities in Southeast Asia in this period, but the truth is that both countries played only a minor role in the area's history. The people of Acheh and then the Bugis were the dominant political and military powers. The Indians and Chinese controlled the bulk of Southeast Asian trade. The Europeans were a colorful group, but their impact was small at this time.

The British had trouble getting their share of business, although they went as far north as Japan. This failure was due to the incompetence of the men sent to make trade surveys and to a lack of enthusiasm in the British East India Company, which was more interested in conquering India than in expanding into Malaya and Indonesia where conflict was sure to arise with the Dutch.

The Rise of Malacca

This situation started to change after Robert Clive—the famous Clive of India—was successful in his Indian aggressions in the middle of the eighteenth century. The conquest of India changed the British East India Company from purely a group of traders to the de facto government of India. Administrative costs of ruling the nation became greater than the East India Company's financial structure could support. This required new markets and new sources of trade revenue. The English had developed a great taste for Chinese tea but could not trade British products for this tea. China had plenty of silk and did not need British woolen and cotton products. Her own ships supplied tin and spices from Indonesia. As a result of the trade imbalance, England was forced to pay in silver for Chinese tea, and silver was in short supply.

Thus England had to expand her trade or see her Eastern empire collapse. As it happened, the empire did not collapse, thanks to a group of swashbuckling men of the type more often found in romantic fiction than in real life.

CHAPTER THREE

The City of the Lion

GREAT Britain was at a disadvantage in the China trade. There were no British-controlled ports her captains could put into on the long sail from India to China and back. Malacca had served as an excellent halfway port under Malay control, but both the Portuguese and the Dutch were British rivals, and foreign ships were not welcome under their regimes. As the China trade increased in importance, so did the need for a British port in the Malay area. There was also a need to open new markets for British products which the Chinese did not want. These British products could be traded in Malaya for such things as tin, damar (a varnish base), and rattan which the Chinese would accept. Such barter would conserve English silver which the East India Company needed to pay for Chinese tea.

A couple of attempts were made to open ports in Borneo, but they quickly failed. Then Francis Light, first of the British adventurers to leave his permanent mark on Malay history, founded a port on Penang, an island off the west coast of Kedah in northern Malaya. Light was an illegitimate child who came to India and Southeast Asia because he had no prospects at home. He started as a private trader in his own ship and then joined the East India Company. One of the arguments advanced by

Light for a port on Penang was that it would make a good naval base to protect East India Company ships on the China trade run.

Light began negotiations with the Sultan of Kedah as early as 1771 for use of Penang, then uninhabited, as a British trading center. The original request was refused, but in 1785 Kedah was threatened by both Siam in the north and the Bugis in Sengalor in central Malaya. The sultan, fearful of being destroyed by one or the other of his enemies, offered Penang Island to Light in exchange for a British guarantee to aid him if attacked by Siam or any of the other Malay sultanates.

Light was eager to make the trade, but the British Foreign Office in London was afraid of becoming entangled in another colonial war at this time. Britain had just lost her American colonies. She was still involved in fighting in India, and had started a conquest of Burma. A war with the Netherlands had just ended and already Britain faced another one with France. Assistance to Kedah against Siam might well cause Siam to join Burma in trying to stop the British conquest in that country. The stakes were too great to risk opening a struggle on a new front.

Still there was no denying that a base was badly needed both to protect ships on the China run and to seek local trade in Malayan tin. This double pressure caused the Foreign Office in London to agree reluctantly to the acquisition of Penang. However, there was a flat prohibition against promising to come to Kedah's aid if attacked. The Sultan of Kedah refused to sign a treaty unless the guarantee was included. Light, a man in the tradition of British colonizers, marched troops into Kedah and forced the sultan to sign.

Penang, despite its promise, never prospered greatly. Two factors worked against it. One was the founding of the great port of Singapore in 1819. And the other was the development of a market for Indian opium in China. This drug was in such demand that in a short time the balance of trade shifted so that it was China who could not supply enough trade to balance the imports and had to start paying silver herself.

The Chinese government realized the danger of opium but was powerless to stop its import. (Years later—in 1840—she did ban the import of the "foreign mud," but was forced to withdraw the ban when Great Britain won "The Opium War" with China, 1839–1842.)

Events in Europe suddenly took a dramatic turn and the effect of the upheaval was felt in Malaya as well. In 1789 the French Revolution shook Europe. The new republic immediately found itself attacked by other countries whose kings did not approve of the French king being beheaded along with his queen. They feared such heresy might spread if left unpunished. The bloody revolutionary government came to an end in 1794 when the tyrant Robespierre was overthrown. The government of France was taken over by a Convention which ruled so poorly that 30,000 guardsmen revolted with the intention of restoring the monarchy. A little-known officer named Napoleon Bonaparte, utilizing only 4,500 men in the face of nearly seven-to-one odds, saved the republic. In November 1799 Napoleon seized power as First Consul of France and in 1804 had himself crowned Emperor of France. Napoleon's rise to power started the Napoleonic Wars in which Great Britain and a few allies tried to stop Napoleon's conquest of all Europe.

French naval bases were too far from Malaya to cause British shipping much damage. However, France overran the Netherlands. The Dutch king fled to England where he asked Great Britain to take Dutch possessions in Southeast Asia to prevent their falling to the French. English sailors stationed in India took Malacca, the Spice Islands, and Djakarta on Java.

Back in Europe, Napoleon suffered a disastrous defeat in attacking Moscow in the winter of 1812. Then two years later he was forced to abdicate as Emperor of France, and the French monarchy was restored under Louis XVIII. The Netherlands then asked Great Britain to withdraw from Dutch territory in the Far East. The British East India Company objected, for it had difficulty competing with the hard business practices of the Dutch traders. The company asked the British Foreign Office to retain Malacca and the Molucca Spice Islands. The request was turned down. Britain still feared France and wanted the Netherlands as an ally in the event of another war with France.

The return of the Dutch left Britain with only Penang as a base in Malaya, and Penang was too far off the regular trade routes to enjoy much prosperity. Navigation had improved so that

The City of the Lion

ships no longer had to hug the coastline. They took a more direct route across the Indian Ocean, bypassing Penang. This made establishment of a new British base in Malaya imperative. Britain particularly wanted a base between Sumatra and Malaya. This would give her control of the shipping lanes as effective as that of Gibraltar over Mediterranean Sea trade.

The man who found the site and a way to get around international objection to it was Thomas Stamford Raffles, the most famous English name in Malaysia's history.

"Stamford Raffles was born on shipboard off the island of Jamaica on July 5th, 1781," writes Charles Burton Buckley in his one-hundred-and-three-year-old book, *An Anecdotal History of Old Times in Singapore*. The book was based on files of the *Singapore Free Press*, which Buckley edited, and on what he was told by men he knew who had been in Singapore. "His father was one of the oldest captains in the West India trade, sailing out of London." After two years in a boarding school, Raffles was placed at the age of fourteen "as a clerk in the large offices of the Honorable East India Company in Leadenhall Street, in the City of London, where the vast political and commercial interests of the East India Company were supervised from England."

The boy seemed to have had a vision of his future destiny as a colonizer in Southeast Asia, for Buckley says that Raffles spent his time off duty studying languages. In 1805 the company decided to increase the staff at Penang, and Raffles, now twenty-four, was selected for the position of assistant secretary of the trading station. On the voyage over he taught himself to speak the Malay language, working from a Malay grammar written by William Marsden, who had spent eight years in Java. This facility for language gave Raffles an advantage over other members of the East India Company staff who for the most part preferred to deal through interpreters rather than take the trouble to learn the language themselves.

Raffles quickly made a name for himself in the company and was personally picked by Lord Minto, Governor-General of India, to govern Java during the British occupation of Batavia, the capital of Dutch Indonesia during the Napoleonic War. This tour lasted from 1811 to 1816 when plans were completed to implement the British-Dutch agreement of 1814 and return Java, Malacca, and the Moluccas to control of the Netherlands.

According to Buckley, "When Raffles left Batavia [present-day Djakarta, Indonesia] the sea roads were filled with boats, crowded with people of all nationalities, who came to see his departure. The deck of his vessel was quite covered with fruits and flowers and offerings of every description . . . the people declaring that Java had lost the greatest friend she had ever possessed."

Raffles's fame penetrated even to Europe. Surprisingly, he stopped at the Island of St. Helena on his way back to England and asked to see Napoleon, who was in exile there following his decisive defeat by the Duke of Wellington at Waterloo. The former Emperor of France had been refusing to see visitors, but he received Raffles and showed great interest in Java. After leaving St. Helena, Raffles went to London, where he was knighted for his work in Java. He returned to Indonesia in October 1816 as Lieutenant-Governor of Bencoolen, the British station on Sumatra.

Bencoolen, a small station on the south of Sumatra, was dominated by the important Dutch station at Palembang. Expansion was impossible and Raffles petitioned the East India Company to let him find a better location for a station. Permission was granted over the almost violent objections of the Lieutenant-Governor of Penang, who viewed the establishment of a new station as the death blow to his port. One of Raffles's strict orders was that the new location would in no way infringe on Dutch territory or involve Great Britain and the Netherlands in any international friction. The Dutch, familiar with Raffles's often unorthodox methods, viewed this new mission with apprehension.

Raffles set sail with Major William Farquhar, who until November 1818 had been Lieutenant-Governor of Malacca. Relieved of duty when the Dutch reassumed command at Malacca, Farquhar was about to return to England when he received an invitation to join Raffles. Later Farquhar claimed partial credit for selecting the Singapore site for the settlement, but a letter written by Raffles to William Marsden before setting sail told his old friend that "my next letter may be dated from the site of the ancient city of Singhapura."

The City of the Lion

The island of Singhapura turned out to be a 224-square-mile body of land at the very tip of the Malay Peninsula. At the time Raffles selected it to be his settlement, the island had only a few Malays under the direct government of the temenggong of Johore. Apparently the island was little known, for Raffles wrote a friend in Europe: "But for my studies, I should hardly have known that such a place existed; not only the European, but the Indian world was also ignorant of it. It is my intention to devote the remaining years of my stay in the East to the advancement of a Colony which, in every way in which it can be viewed, bids fair to be one of the most important . . . which we possess . . . Our object is not territory but trade; a great commercial emporium and a fulcrum, whence we may extend our influence politically as circumstances may hereafter require. By taking immediate possession, we put a negative to the Dutch claim of exclusion, and, at the same time, revive the drooping confidence of our allies and friends. One free port in these seas must eventually destroy the spell of Dutch monopoly."

It was as if Raffles were looking into a crystal ball when he wrote this letter to the Duchess of Somerset in England, for it all came true. However, before this could happen, Raffles had to settle the touchy question of legal title to the island in such a manner that the British government would approve the settlement. The early history of the island is, as one historian puts it, very obscure. We have nothing but legends, and the legends contradict each other. K. G. Tregonning, Raffles Professor of History, University of Singapore, quotes the partly legendary story of Paramesvara, the fugitive from Indonesia, who supposedly settled at Tumasik—the site of the modern city of Singapore—before going on to found Malacca in the late fourteenth century.

On the other hand, Buckley has this legend in his book: "It is said . . . that Sang Nila Utama settled on the island with a colony of Malays from Palembang in Sumatra and founded the city of Singhapura in A.D. 1160, when they changed the original name of Tumasik to Singhapura." This implies that the settlement existed two hundred years before the date given by Tregonning and that there was a settlement there before the Malays arrived. Another source gives the settlement date as A.D. 1260. In any event, they all agree on the meaning of the name.

In Sanskrit, *Singha* means lion and *pura* is city. Singapore, then, is the Anglicized form of Singhapura or "The City of the Lion." Buckley quotes a legend to the effect that Singhapura's founder saw a lion near the mouth of the Singapore River which caused him to pick this name for his settlement. Later historians point out that lions are not found in Malaya. It is possible that Buckley's Sang Nila Utama saw a stone lion left from the ruins of a previous city on this site.

An account of Raffles's founding of Singapore is found in *The Hakayit of Abdulla,* written by Munshi (teacher) Abdulla, who was Raffles's clerk. Abdulla's great-grandfather was an Arab who married a Malay woman. The rest of Abdulla's ancestry is Malay. His father was the scholar who taught Malay to William Marsden, whose grammar text Raffles used to study the language. Abdulla was a brilliant lad and by the time he was twelve was employed by Raffles in translating Malay documents into English.

Later when Raffles founded Singapore he sent for Abdulla to come from Malacca. He needed a trustworthy translator for the difficult negotiations because he wanted a legal title to the island.

British colonial adventurers were not always so eager to obtain legal title to their conquests. However, Raffles faced a trying international situation. He had to consider Dutch reaction to a British settlement at Singapore. For more than a hundred years traders from the Netherlands had dominated Southeast Asian trade, and the British government in London would not take kindly to any colonial action that alienated the Netherlands. It was imperative that any British settlement, *at this time,* be on land unclaimed by the Dutch. It was well known that Raffles hated the Dutch, and they had mutual feelings about him. During the Napoleonic Wars when Britain had occupied much of the Dutch colonial empire, Raffles worked hard to ensure permanent English occupation and then bitterly opposed turning the settlements back to Dutch control under the treaty of 1814.

Raffles's first goal was the island of Rhio south of Singapore. But the Dutch, getting wind of his intention, moved onto the island. This may have been a feint, since Raffles had earlier written Marsden that Singapore was his goal. When Raffles

A bronze statue of Stamford Raffles in front of Victoria Memorial Hall in Singapore. The eyes of the statue are said to be looking directly at the spot where Sir Stamford first landed on the island in 1819.

landed in Singapore, the island was inhabited by 150 Malays who had come from Johore state with the Viceroy of Johore. The viceroy told Raffles that the island had been given to him. No reason has been given why so high an official should have left the capital and come to such a deserted island. The supposition is that he found it expedient to get away from Johore for a while. In addition to the Malays from Johore, there were a number of *orang laut*—men of the sea—who lived with their families on boats in the coves of the island. These hereditary sailors lived by fishing and piracy.

The ruler welcomed Raffles, assuring the Englishman that he would welcome a British settlement. There was a major difficulty, however. Though the viceroy owned the island, it nevertheless came under the suzerainty of the Sultan of Johore. This in turn presented a new complication. The sultan had recently died and the succession to his throne was in question.

The oldest son and acknowledged heir, Hussein, was away in Pahang state when his father died, and the monsoon had delayed his return. The dead sultan's temenggong, Rajah Muda Japhar, had quarreled with Hussein and feared his return. Japhar forced the council to accept Hussein's younger half-brother Abdul Rahman as sultan. Raffles learned that the Viceroy of Singapore was loyal to Hussein and was an enemy of Japhar, who actually ruled through the weak sultan, Abdul Rahman.

Raffles decided that Hussein had the stronger legal claim to the throne of Johore. He picked two trusted Malays as his emissaries to treat secretly with Hussein, who was now in exile on the Dutch-held island of Rhio. The Malays used an *orang laut* pirate chief to smuggle them into the island without Dutch knowledge. They presented Raffles's plan to make Hussein the Sultan of Johore and, when Hussein agreed, smuggled him out of Dutch control. They returned to Singapore with the sultan-to-be on February 1, 1819.

Singapore was a very desolate place at that time. Munshi Abdulla tells us that the harbor at the mouth of the Singapore River had only a small clearing with less than fifty huts and a house that served as the viceroy's palace. As for the general location, the Arab-Malay writer said: "No man dared to pass through the Straits of Singapore; jinns and satans even were afraid, for that was the place the pirates made use of to sleep and to divide their plunder. There also they put their captives to death and killed each other in quarrels over their spoils. All along the beach there were hundreds of human skulls, some of them fresh with the hair still remaining, some with the teeth still sharp..."

Raffles knew that even deposed rulers loved pomp and ceremony. So he had his sailors cut trees to make a clearing and a tent was pitched here to receive the sultan-to-be. When Hussein landed, Raffles had bolts of red trade goods stretched across the sand to make a red carpet for him to walk on.

Negotiations went well. In exchange for British recognition of his position as Sultan of Johore, Hussein granted Raffles the right to establish a factory (trading post) on Singapore Island. In addition Raffles promised Hussein an annual pension of $5,000 and protection of the British Army as long as the trading agreement was in force. (The dollars to be paid were Straits dollars and were worth about fifty cents U.S. each at that time. Today the Singapore dollar is worth about twenty-eight cents U.S.)

As soon as the treaty with Hussein was concluded, Raffles returned to Bencoolen, his headquarters on Sumatra. William Farquhar was left with the monumental job of turning one tent and a cleared area into a trading center. Farquhar went to work, surrounded by pirates and under threat of a Dutch attack to drive him out. His troubles were compounded by a running feud that developed between himself and Raffles. Both were able men, but their basic philosophies differed. Raffles insisted that his orders be carried out exactly as he gave them, while Farquhar—an army officer who distrusted civilians—felt that he knew the problems better than his absentee master in Bencoolen.

Most historians side with Raffles. However, Tregonning has this to say in his book, *The British in Malaya:* "One of the clues to this ambitious, impetuous and clever man is his size; Raffles was of small stature. Like most small men, he endeavored to make up for what he lacked by a fierce watching of rights, by self assertion; he took umbrage very quickly."

Raffles's action caused consternation in London. There was

fear that his high-handed dealings as a sultan-maker would involve Britain and the Netherlands in a colonial war. As expected, the Dutch government protested vigorously. It claimed a trade treaty with Sultan Abdul Rahman included Singapore. Raffles countered with a treaty Farquhar had signed with Abdul Rahman giving the British trade rights in Johore in 1818, before Dutch territory was returned by the British following the Napoleonic Wars. Raffles now claimed he had legal sanction from both rulers; the legal ruler Hussein whom the British supported, and the usurper Abdul Rahman whom the Dutch supported.

The British Foreign Office in London protested that Raffles and Farquhar would be overwhelmed by a Dutch attack, but Lord Hastings, Viceroy in India, supported Raffles. While the Foreign Office vacillated, unable to make a concrete decision, the threat diminished. If the politicians back in London were fearful of Singapore's future, traders in the Far East were not. Within four months of Raffles's initial landing, Singapore had grown from its original 150 Malays to a population of five thousand. Within a year the population doubled again and business was totaling four million Straits dollars annually. Singapore was well on its way to becoming what it is today: the most important seaport in Southeast Asia and the fourth largest in the world.

Several factors worked to Singapore's advantage from the start. One was its excellent harbor and perfect location in the center of the water roads between the mainland and the islands of Indonesia. Another was the reputation for fairness in dealing with all traders which Raffles had won in his previous work in Bencoolen and Malacca. Still another that aided Singapore's rapid growth was free trade. Penang charged a 5 percent duty on all goods imported. Although Tregonning claims that Raffles permitted duty-free trade "half-heartedly" with the intention of adding a duty as soon as trade was established, Buckley quotes a letter Raffles wrote to a group of "European and Native Merchants of Singapore," who expressed fear when Raffles prepared to return to England in 1823:

"That Singapore will long and always remain a Free Port, and that no taxes on trade or industry will be established to check its future rise and prosperity, I can have no doubt. I am justified in saying thus much, on the authority of the Supreme Government in India and on the authority of those who are most likely to have weight in the councils of our nation at home."

The majority of the newcomers to Singapore were Chinese, establishing a Chinese majority that continues to the present day with 75 percent of the population being Chinese. Abdulla has left a description of Singapore's trade during the first two years of the colony's operation:

"Every day the quantity of goods for sale increased. It is impossible to describe the wonderful variety of the goods brought for sale by the Europeans, such as our fathers had never seen before. Auctions were held constantly where the goods were sold wonderfully cheap. At that time the auctioneer's gongs were not beaten, nor was notice sent around. The custom was simply to paste up notices at the several street corners that tomorrow at 10 o'clock an auction would be held at Mr. So-and-so's house, with a list of the articles for sale."

Abdulla then goes on to describe the city in the second and third years of its existence: "The houses were all attap [palm thatch] except the one built of brick by Mr. McSweeney who soon afterwards returned to England and it was then used for a police station. There was not a single house on the other side of the river. It was a mangrove swamp and all lived on the Plain side of the river."

Raffles made periodic visits to Singapore to check up on Farquhar, with whom relations were growing worse. After one of these visits Raffles reported that during the first two and a half years of the settlement's existence, 2,889 vessels had cleared the port, handling $8,568,172 in business.

Singapore was rapidly becoming the most important port in Southeast Asia.

CHAPTER FOUR

Life in Early Singapore

THE LAND ceded to the British East India Company was at first sold to traders. Then Raffles decided that he had made a mistake. The sales contracts were canceled and ninety-nine-year leases were substituted. To prevent hard feelings, Raffles canceled all rents and lease fees for the full ninety-nine years to those few who had sales contracts canceled. This fairness characterized all of his intercourse with everyone except those who worked for him. With his subordinates he became increasingly tyrannical. In 1820, smarting under a fancied grievance, he removed harbor control from Farquhar and placed it under Raffles Flint, his nephew, whom all except Raffles thought incompetent.

Abdulla mentions an incident to show how far Raffles would go to support one of his ideas. Farquhar and Raffles got into an argument over which side of the river should be developed into the mercantile center. Farquhar favored the side on which they had landed, but Raffles thought it should be on the swampy side. Raffles agreed that it would be extremely expensive either to fill the swamp or to build the stores on pile foundations. However, he pointed out that if he let merchants build on the good side of the river, the other side would not be settled for a hundred years.

Raffles gathered up three hundred Chinese coolies and put

Life in Early Singapore

them to work tearing down a hill back of Singapore. The dirt was carried in baskets on their backs and dumped into the swamp. Abdulla says, "Mr. Raffles came twice a day to give directions. After about three or four months the hill was completely cut down, and all the hollows and streams of the swamp filled. After the marshy land was filled up, raised, and embanked, it was measured out into lots and sold by auction.

"Mr. Raffles advised me to buy four or five lots, as afterwards this part of town would be valuable. I answered where could I get money enough to pay for land. I saw the lots selling for $1,200. Mr. Raffles smiled and said, never mind the money, take the land first and we'll talk about the payment later."

Abdulla said frankly that he did not expect Singapore to succeed and turned down the offer. Later he learned that none of those who bid on the property ever paid for it. Raffles arranged for the big prices to keep out "paupers," as Abdulla calls them, who would have flocked in if they had known the land was free.

While the hill was being leveled to fill the swamp, the diggers found a curious rock. It had been flattened on one side and carved with some lettering. The lettering was worn so badly that it could not be deciphered. In fact, no one could be sure what language it was written in. Raffles insisted that it was Hindu simply because this Indian race was the first in the area who were capable of writing. The Chinese claimed it was Chinese writing, but that not enough remained to tell what was written. Abdulla said that it looked more like Arabic to him.

Raffles was an antiquarian and had written a book on the history of Java. He was much interested in the stone, for he intended also to write a history of Malaya. He had the stone washed with acid, rubbed with a dark substance, and viewed by slanted light. All attempts to make the inscription legible failed. A description of the rock claimed it was of red sandstone and contained about fifty lines of writing. Raffles hoped that it would eventually shed light on the past history of Singapore. However, the stone was eventually broken up and cut into slabs of building stone. The original stone was said to have been about nine by ten feet in height and width, and two to three feet thick.

Years later a naval officer, studying an early translation of the

Malay Annals, found three stories connected with stones in the Singapore area. The first two dealt with people who were turned to stone in a miraculous manner. But the third seemed to explain the mysterious Singapore stone. The Rajah of Singapore had in his retinue a famous strong man named Badang. In Kling, India (now Coromandel), the king heard of Badang and sent his own champion to challenge the strong man. The rajah and the Indian king bet seven ships on the result. The test was made by raising a great rock near the rajah's palace. The Indian raised it to his knees and let it drop. Badang raised the rock above his head and threw it into the mouth of the Singapore River, "where it remained ever after." The rajah was so delighted that when Badang died he had two stone pillars inscribed and placed as a monument over the strong man's grave. The officer believed that the mysterious Singapore stone was one of these inscriptions.

Another reminder that Singapore was once an important place is the ruins of a fortress wall ten feet thick which was found in one place. According to a story told by John Cameron, editor of the famous newspaper *Straits Times* a hundred years ago, the city these walls guarded fell because of treachery sometime about A.D. 1250. The kings of Java made several unsuccessful attempts to take the city but were defeated every time. Then the prince who ruled the city married the beautiful daughter of his viceroy. The prince's other wives were jealous of the lovely girl and soon accused her of infidelity. The angry ruler ordered the girl impaled on swords. The viceroy pleaded for his innocent daughter's life. When this failed, he begged for a less degrading death for her. This too was refused and the girl was slain. The bitter father secretly contacted the Javanese and opened the citadel's gates to them in the night. The city was destroyed.

In January 1823 Raffles wrote the East India Company in Calcutta asking to be relieved for reasons of poor health. At the same time he wrote an entire page insisting that Colonel Farquhar (who had been promoted from major to lieutenant colonel by the British Army) was incompetent and should not succeed him. Farquhar, however, continued as Resident (governor) of Singapore under Raffles's Bencoolen command until May. At

Life in Early Singapore

that time Raffles relieved Farquhar of command because the subordinate had sent a report to India instead of to Raffles.

Without detracting from Raffles's accomplishments, many historians and writers feel that Farquhar was ill treated by the domineering Raffles. Farquhar was in command of Singapore for its first four years and deserves as much credit as Raffles for its outstanding success. Farquhar returned to England and died in 1839 as a major general in the British Army. Although his accomplishments have been overshadowed by those of Stamford Raffles, in the history of Singapore he must be given his place on the roll of great pioneers.

There is absolutely no doubt that Stamford Raffles was an enlightened ruler. The regard the natives felt for him is apparent in their actions both when he left Bencoolen and later when he left Singapore. His draft for a constitution for Singapore shows his insistence upon fair play for all races within his jurisdiction. The first part of his "Proclamation of Laws" pointed out the different backgrounds of the Malays and Chinese who made up the bulk of Singapore's population and how this background differed from that of Europeans. "Under these conditions," he wrote, "it is not always possible to apply the laws of Europe direct."

In general he said, "Nothing should be endured in the Settlement, however sanctioned by local useage of particular tribes, that has a direct or a notoriously strong tendency to endanger the safety or liberty of person or the security of property." He went on to enumerate such basic laws as honest weights and measures, prohibition against frauds, sanctity of oaths, prohibition against imprisonment for debts, etc.

Raffles's character and his differences from so many early colonial administrators are shown in the way he explained the need for changes he was forced to make in local customs and laws. One such change was the age-old Malay tradition of redressing a wrong by slaying one's enemy. "It ought to be understood," Raffles said, "that while individuals are allowed to *protect* themselves against wrongs, the *redress* of wrongs cannot be left to the resentment or revenge of the parties conceiving themselves injured.

"Therefore, no one being allowed to revenge his own case,

arms or weapons capable of inflicting instant death as worn habitually by the Malays become unnecessary. By dispensing with them, the greatest temptation to end the power of doing to others the greatest and irremediable wrong in depriving them of life is in a great measure removed."

Raffles went on to tell how if one accused a neighbor of stealing a cow and later found the neighbor was innocent, redress could be made for the error; but if one takes the life of a fellow man in anger, nothing can bring back that life if the killer should later find he was wrong.

In the clause on prohibition of gambling, Raffles also went out of his way to explain the need for the law instead of telling his subjects that they *would* stop betting on game cocks.

Later in the document he wrote: "The constitution of England defines the absolute rights of the subject as follows:

"1st. The right of personal security. 2nd. The right of personal liberty. And 3rdly. The right of property.

"There seems to be no reason for denying corresponding rights to all classes of people residing under the protection of the British flag at Singapore.

"Let all men be considered equal in the eye of the law.

"Let no man be banished from the country without a trial by his peers.

"Let no man be deprived of his liberty without a cause, and no man detained in confinement beyond 48 hours without a right to demand a trial according to due course of law."

Raffles was also guilty of some rather peculiar legal ideas. In one place he wrote that the purpose of laws was to secure legal obligations, and that they must never transcend moral obligations. "The English practice of teaching prisoners to plead not guilty, that they may have a chance of escaping from punishment, is inconsistent with this aim and consequently objectionable."

Raffles's successor was John Crawfurd. Crawfurd had been in the Bengal (India) Medical Service and later served as civil surgeon in Penang. He was a very cold person and quite coolly regarded by the people of Singapore, who had liked Raffles and Farquhar very much. Abdulla wrote of him: "His impatience prevented him from listening to long complaints, and he did not care to investigate matters. As sure as there was a plaint he would cut it short in the middle. On this account I have heard that most people murmured and were dissatisfied, feeling that they could not accept his decision with good will, but by force only."

Raffles left Singapore in June 1823 for Bencoolen, from where he embarked for England with his wife and infant child on the ship *Fame*. Both he and his wife were in poor health and several of their children had died in Southeast Asia. Shortly after departure a torch carried by a steward drawing brandy from the ship's supply caused a fire that destroyed the ship. Raffles and his family escaped in small boats and returned to Bencoolen, but all their property was lost. The greatest loss was historical. In Raffles's own words:

"The loss I have to regret, above all, is my papers and drawings; all my notes and observations; my intended account of the establishment of Singapore; Eastern grammars, dictionaries, and vocabularies; and all my collection of natural history."

Additional information about the loss comes from Abdulla, who wrote: "When I heard the news I was breathless, remembering all the Malay books of ancient date collected from various sources; all these lost. As to Mr. Raffles's other property I did not care, for, if his life was spared, he could reinstate this. But the books could not be recovered, for none of them were printed but were in manuscript; they were so rare. I further remembered his intention of composing a work on these countries, and his promise to put my name in it. All these are gone."

The loss was a great blow not only to history but also to science, for the collection contained over two thousand drawings of rare plants and animals of Southeast Asia. It had been Raffles's intention to spend his retirement using this material in a collection of histories of Malaya, Borneo, and Sumatra to follow his previously published history of Java.

He immediately booked passage on another ship, but the captain went mad before it could sail. He took still another and finally departed, arriving in England in August 1824. He spent the next two years arguing with directors of the East India Company in London about sums due him, and then he died on July 5, 1826. He was forty-five years old. "A young age," Buckley wrote, "for one who had done so much for the good of all around him, and for his fellow countrymen after him."

High-level talks between the British and the Dutch over Raffles's occupation of Singapore began in 1819 soon after the Dutch learned of the landing. By 1823 Singapore had proven so valuable that the British had no intention of leaving, regardless of what action the Dutch took. The only dissenters were the merchants and governor of Penang whose business fell off drastically as trade bypassed the older island settlement and came to Singapore.

The discussions finally ended in the Anglo-Dutch treaty of 1824. In effect, the two countries drew a line along the equator. Territory above the line was reserved for English influence. Below the line was the Dutch sphere of influence. The East India Company withdrew from Bencoolen on Sumatra in accordance with this treaty. The Dutch gave up some harbors in India and the port of Malacca. The trade benefited both sides. Bencoolen had never done much trade since the Dutch at Batavia (now Djakarta, Java) got the lion's share. The English had retained only Bencoolen because of some valuable pepper plantations there. On the other hand, the Dutch had never made any money out of Malacca. The harbor was silting up so badly that ships had difficulty getting in. So each side got rid of its white elephants in the deal. From the British point of view the valuable prize was Dutch acknowledgment of British sovereignty in Singapore. At the same time John Crawfurd, Raffles's successor, negotiated a new treaty with the Sultan of Johore which ceded the entire island to Great Britain. Raffles's treaty had provided for space to build only a trading settlement.

Since the Indian headquarters of the East India Company could not govern its far-flung commercial empire from India, sections of that empire were broken into "Presidencies." Each Presidency was maintained by a lieutenant-governor responsible to the governor of the East India Company in Calcutta, India. It is important to remember that the East India Company began as a private enterprise and did not become government-controlled until the end of its long operations. The actions of the company and its men were the actions of private individuals. However, as in the case of official British government reaction to Raffles's territorial encroachment, the company's actions and expansions had to coincide with official policy. Otherwise Great Britain might find herself involved in a war.

The private nature of the East India Company also explains why Great Britain did not—as the Dutch did—seize territorial and political control of all areas where their trade settlements were located. The British did grab total control in India, but once this was done, the company had to bear the costs of administering the new acquisition in the years before the Indian government was taken over by the British crown. The costs were enormous. The purpose of the East India Company was to make money—not to pay it out governing countries.

This policy is what kept the Malay Peninsula independent in the fifty years following the settlement of Singapore. British direct control extended only to Singapore Island, Penang Island, and the small state of Malacca which surrounded the city and port. These three areas were combined into a Presidency, governed first from Penang and then from Singapore. In the 1830s these areas became known as the Straits Settlements to differentiate them from the rest of Malaya.

The rest of Malaya was divided into states and sultanates. Ordinarily a state was governed by a rajah who owed allegiance of varying degrees to a sultan who—at least in name—governed one or more states. At the time the Anglo-Dutch treaty was signed in 1824, the peninsula was controlled mainly by the Johore Sultanate, the Thais from Siam who had influence over several northern Malay states, and the independent state of Negri Sembilan north of Malacca.

The Siamese had been trying to add the peninsula to their territory for more than four hundred years. Kelantan, a large state on the east coast, was created from a number of petty states and became a sultanate in 1800 under nominal Siamese suzerainty. Trengganu, on the east coast south of Kelantan, sent tribute to both the Siamese and the Sultan of Riau, the Dutch-controlled archipelago. The Riau Sultanate also claimed suzerainty over Pahang, the central and largest of the Malay peninsular states at this time. Kedah, on the west coast opposite Penang, was completely under Siamese control. Perak, south of Kedah, was independent and was ruled by the last of the line of old Malaccan sultans.

There was a misunderstanding over how far Dutch territory extended inland from the city of Malacca. When the British took over Malacca in 1825, this area was controlled by the tiny state of Naning. Difficulties arose and a war resulted which ended in the annexation of Naning to Malacca, enlarging the port city-state to the size of the present state of Malacca. The war, while successful militarily, cost the East India Company so much money that critics used it as an example of why the British should keep away from territorial expansion and confine themselves strictly to trade settlements. This again became the policy. Great Britain and the East India Company paid little attention to the internal activities of the Malay states unless Great Britain had some direct involvement.

In the meantime Singapore continued to grow in importance. By 1830 the city's port was doing more than twice the business of Penang and Malacca combined. Settlement of the British-Dutch trouble brought fifty years of peace which greatly aided trade expansion. While the British were content to sit on their conquests, the Dutch were rapidly expanding through the Indonesian area. Although Britain and the East India Company were content with maintaining the status quo, individual Englishmen were not. This attitude brought to Southeast Asia a remarkable man and one of the most colorful of the swashbuckling adventurers who did so much for the British Empire during its years of imperialistic expansion. James Brooke, the "White Rajah of Sarawak," came to the area in his private ship, made himself ruler of a private kingdom, and founded a dynasty that ruled until World War II. He was the kind of man who appears more often in fiction than in real life.

CHAPTER FIVE

The White Rajah

JAMES BROOKE, who became the white rajah, was born in India where his father was a civil service judge for the East India Company. He was sent to England to be educated when he was twelve but was not a successful scholar. He was permitted to return to India in 1819 when he was sixteen to join the 6th Native Infantry as an ensign. He was thrilled to hear of Stamford Raffles's conquest of Singapore. Right then was born his own dream of pushing back the frontier of the British Empire in the Orient. James was unhappy with his assignment of Sub-Assistant Commissary General. He felt he was fitted for better things than furnishing subsistence to the Army. But his work kept him busy. And at the moment there was little James could do about his ambition.

His big chance came in 1825. Lord Amherst, Governor-General of Bengal Province, learned from native spies that Burma was plotting a surprise attack on British headquarters in Calcutta. In late 1824 Amherst declared war against Burma to forestall the Burmese invasion. Brooke got into battle in January 1825 and displayed such bravery that he was "mentioned in dispatches." This is the way the British commend acts below those meriting an actual medal for heroism. Being mentioned in dispatches was and still is an honor and often puts the recipient in line for promotion.

Brooke was now working with the cavalry. In order to get out of the infantry commissary job, he volunteered to raise a troop of light cavalry for reconnaissance and scouting. Several days after his first fight, Brooke's scout troop again contacted the enemy. There was a pitched battle. Brooke was shot and left for dead but later was picked up and survived. The bullet, which had lodged near his spine, was taken from his body and sent to England, where it was kept by his mother as a souvenir. She displayed it in a glass case in the Brooke parlor.

James received a three-and-a-half-year convalescent leave. As he was returning to India to resume his commission, his ship was wrecked and his health relapsed. He again recovered and started back once more. However, his time was running out. James was not commissioned in the British Army. He was in the East India Company's private army. Company regulations required anyone whose leave of absence was longer than five years to forfeit his commission. James knew he could not get back to Calcutta on time. He put in to Madras on the southeast Indian coast and asked to be temporarily enrolled in the Madras Division of the Army so he could be carried on the rolls before the five years elapsed. His request was refused. He turned his back on the Army and took passage on a ship that went to Penang, then to Singapore, and finally to Canton, China.

James returned to England, on fire to become a trader. He persuaded his father, who had since retired in England, to buy him a ship, but James and the ship's captain quarreled. As a result the voyage was a failure and the cargo had to be sold at a loss. Young Brooke came back to England, where his father died in 1835. The son's share of his father's estate was about the equivalent of $150,000 in U.S. currency. James immediately bought a 142-ton schooner with six 6-pound cannon and a number of swivel guns capable of beating off pirates.

His intention was to avoid conflict with other traders by opening new territory. For some time he had been considering Borneo as the base of his operations. This large island east of the Malay Peninsula had some minor Dutch settlements in the south, but the north had no trading centers at all. The British twice tried to make settlements there but failed both times.

Borneo lies four hundred miles east of Singapore and is the

largest land mass on the Sunda Platform. It stretches more than six hundred miles from northern tip to southern tip and is cut by the equator. It is hilly and mountainous. The mountains of the north are part of the long range that forms the Philippine Islands north of Borneo. The largest part of the island, even today, is so choked with rain forest that no human beings live there except for a scattering of wandering aborigine tribes. What settlements there were had been established on the narrow alluvial plains and around the mouths of the rivers.

Borneo has no written history. The distant past was a complete blank until around 1954 when diggers harvesting bat guano in some huge limestone caves near Niah in north Sarawak discovered remarkable prehistoric remains. "Among the finds were the almost-perfect skeletons of small people with beautifully made and polished stone axes and adzes lying among them," writes Harry Miller, a historian. "Wall paintings in red haematite [iron ore] on the limestone wall of another cave and some fragile relics are believed to date back to 50,000 B.C." The curtain drops here and nothing else is known about Borneo until A.D. 600 when it is mentioned in Chinese records. Some historians interpret earlier Chinese documents as referring to Borneo, but such references are so vague as to be subject to differing interpretations.

The aborigine tribes still represented in Borneo today are kin to the Malays and show their Mongoloid origin. The largest of the aborigine groups is the Dayaks. Dayak is a Malay word meaning "savage" and was indiscriminately applied to all aborigine people by the first Europeans coming into Borneo. Later the natives were classified as Sea Dayaks and Land Dayaks, although they are not the same people. They are, however, ethnically related. Of the two, the Sea Dayaks, originally a ferocious pirate group, gave Europeans the most trouble. The Land Dayaks were shy and wanted only to be left alone. They retreated into the interior as settlers came.

For centuries the entire west coast of Borneo was a pirates' haven. These pirates were not individual free enterprise killers like those of the Western Hemisphere. In Borneo entire tribes and sometimes nations were organized under their sultans to prey on shipping between China and India. Writers of this period were unanimous in calling the Dayaks the most vicious people on earth. A favorite pirate method of attack was to catch a becalmed vessel at night. The Dayaks would row their low boats in close and then swarm onto the deck of the merchantman. All prisoners taken by the pirates who were not slain were sold as slaves or tortured for amusement.

Sometime around A.D. 1500 Malays from the peninsula settled in Brunei in Northwest Borneo. Shortly after this a famous pirate called Sultan Bulkiah seized power. This man, known as *Nakhoda Ragam*—the Singing Captain—brought a large section of Borneo under his rule. Then, swinging north in his conquests, Bulkiah conquered several islands in the Sulu Sea and even sacked Manila in the Philippines. The current name Borneo is a corruption of Brunei and goes back to the sixteenth century when Bulkiah's Sultanate of Brunei controlled most of the big island.

The ships of Ferdinand Magellan, first man to circumnavigate the globe, called at Brunei during the height of its power. Magellan was slain while helping the Sultan of Cebu in a war, but his crew continued the voyage. The expedition's historian, a Portuguese named Pigafetta, told how the voyagers were welcomed to Brunei. The city of Brunei, he wrote, was just a collection of thatched huts "built entirely in the salt water." From this we infer that the buildings were raised on poles along the beach like so many villages found today in Borneo and throughout the South Seas. The sweep of the tide serves as a ready-made means of keeping such a village clean. Such an arrangement is considered more sanitary than a village built on land. An exception to the beach houses in Brunei was the sultan's palace and the homes of his immediate retinue.

Magellan's men were welcomed by the Bruneians and mounted on elephants which took them to the sultan's palace. Pigafetta says they rode right into the building, passing between a guard of three hundred men who stood with drawn swords. The sultan sat on a dais behind a curtain which slaves lifted so he could see the visitors. The foreigners were not allowed to speak to the sultan directly, but spoke to intermediaries who passed the conversation among three of them before it reached the ruler.

After this visit Europeans showed little interest in Borneo

until the end of the sixteenth century, when the Dutch established a settlement on the south end of the island. As time passed most of the island came under Dutch influence. When James Brooke arrived in 1839 nothing remained of the once powerful Brunei sultanate except the northern states of Brunei, Sarawak, and part of Sabah.

Brooke's arrival in Brunei was not accidental. He had learned earlier that there was trouble in the sultanate and he hoped to take advantage of it. Brunei was then under the rule of Sultan Omar Ali. A tribe of Dayaks in Sarawak had rebelled against their governor, a rascal named Makota who was also a relative of the sultan. The sultan sent his deputy, Rajah Muda, to put down the revolt. Muda moved to Kuching, the capital of Sarawak, a miserable, fever-ridden swamp where lived about 1,500 people. He was making no headway at all in containing the revolt when James Brooke arrived in his armed ship. Brooke was the first white man the rajah had ever seen. He had heard of them, however, and nothing he had heard was good. He suspected the Englishman of being a spy. He craftily refused to speak ill of the Dutch and kept asking Brooke which was the more powerful nation, the Netherlands or Great Britain. Brooke gravely assured him that Great Britain was the world's most powerful nation.

The next day Brooke met the crafty Makota, "a real living Dayak of Lundu. The Dayak's complexion was somewhat darker than the average Malay. The countenance intelligent, the eye quick and wandering; the forehead of medium height. His stature was five feet two inches, his limbs were well formed and muscular. He was by no means shy or reserved," Brooke wrote later.

Questioning Makota, Brooke learned that the Dayak was a head hunter, but that he hunted heads only during a war. He *never* went out and cut off heads just for the pleasure, the Dayak explained through an interpreter.

Later Brooke took a hundred-mile boat trip up the Lundu River to visit villages inhabited by Dayaks such as the one he met in Kuching. He traveled by night and wrote of the glorious moon, the dark fringe of the jungle, and "here and there a tree flashing and shining with fireflies." He carried his own camping equipment, but after a sudden rainstorm spent the rest of the night in a native house.

His description of a Borneo "long house" shows how little things have changed in the 132 years since Brooke made his first trip into the Borneo interior. Such communal homes are still to be found among wilder tribes in the back country today.

"There is *one* enormous house for the entire village population. It measures 594 feet in length, and the front room or *street,* is the entire length of the building, and twenty-one feet broad. The back part is divided by mat partitions into private apartments of the various families, and of these there are forty-five separate doors leading to the public apartment. The widowers and young unmarried men occupy the public room, as only those with wives are entitled to the advantage of separate rooms."

He went on to describe the general building. It was raised twelve feet from the ground and the stairway for entry was nothing but a pole in which notches were cut. "A most steep, difficult and awkward ladder," Brooke reported. "In front is a terrace fifty feet long. This platform, as well as the front room, is the resort of pigs, dogs, birds, monkeys and fowls, and presents a glorious scene of confusion and bustle."

On top of the long house was a second-story cache where food and implements were stored. The people slept on cots made from hollow logs, and the place was decorated with thirty skulls, trophies of their head-hunting prowess. The Dayaks did not shrink their captured heads like the Indians of the Amazon in South America, but just retained the skulls. All his life Brooke was to make apologies for the head-hunting activities of his Dayak friends, insisting that they were taken only in time of war and then from fallen foes. No man ever killed just to get a head for a trophy. However, there is evidence that, in some tribes at least, a young man was not permitted to marry until he had taken a head. It is hardly reasonable to believe that he waited for a convenient intertribal war, since bachelorhood was considered unnatural.

On his return from these explorations Brooke again pressed the rajah concerning the fighting in Sarawak. Rajah Muda kept insisting that there was no fighting and that the situation was well under control. Brooke then sailed for other islands, but returned eleven months later on his way to the Philippines and China. He found a very agitated Rajah Muda. The insurrection had gotten completely out of hand, and Muda feared his sultan's wrath. The rajah begged Brooke to help him. This was what the British adventurer had been waiting for. He quickly agreed to help, but found that Muda was strangely reluctant to act on any of the plans he advanced. Finally Brooke threatened to leave. Again Rajah Muda begged the Englishman to stay, even going so far as to promise him the governorship of Sarawak if he would help in the fighting.

Brooke wrote a letter home in which he said that he was not sure that Rajah Muda was serious in his proposal to make him ruler of Sarawak Province, but just the same, the idea appealed to the English adventurer. In the meantime, Muda kept hindering Brooke's efforts to defeat the rebels. Later Brooke discovered that Muda's indecision was caused by Makota who hated the Englishman and worked to change Rajah Muda's mind each time the rajah agreed to Brooke's plans. Finally Brooke went ahead with some of his own men and defeated the rebels.

Brooke now tried to hold Rajah Muda to his promise to make him Rajah (governor) of Sarawak. Muda repeated his promise and drew up an agreement. The agreement, when translated by Brooke, proved to be only an agreement to trade. Muda explained to the angry Englishman that this was done deliberately because Sarawak was a state of the Brunei Sultanate and Sultan Omar Ali would have to approve any transfer of territory. This would be done eventually, Rajah Muda assured Brooke, but it would take some time. Muda claimed that his strategy was to get Omar Ali used to Brooke's presence as a trader before broaching the subject of making the Englishman Rajah of Sarawak.

The dickering and bickering continued until James Brooke lost his temper. His anger was partly at Rajah Muda and partly at Sultan Omar Ali. Omar Ali had thirty shipwrecked Englishmen in captivity and was demanding ransom for them.

What happened next is recorded in Brooke's journal: "Repairing on board my ship, I mustered my people, explained my intentions and mode of operation, and having loaded the vessel's guns and brought her broadside to bear, I proceeded on shore with a detachment fully armed."

Brooke drew up his armed guard in front of the rajah's palace. Gaining an immediate audience with Rajah Muda, Brooke accused Makota of villainy and undermining all the good Brooke had accomplished. Even though he knew that Makota was the relative of both Rajah Muda and Sultan Omar Ali, Brooke informed the frightened Muda that he intended to drive Makota from the country by force.

"I explained to the Rajah," Brooke wrote, "that several chiefs and a large body of Siniawan Dayaks [the rebels Brooke had lately defeated] were ready to assist me, and that the only course left to prevent bloodshed was immediately to proclaim me governor . . . After this demonstration, affairs proceeded cheerily to a conclusion. The Rajah was active in settling; the agreement was drawn, sealed, and signed. Guns fired. Flags waved. And on the 24th September, 1841, I became the Governor of Sarawak with the fullest powers."

Brooke took his new position as Rajah of Sarawak seriously. He immediately set up court in his cottage and began dispensing justice. He kept four Englishmen from the ship to help him in Kuching, the capital of Sarawak. The rest of his men were sent out in two ships to continue trading. Brooke began work to bring law and order to his state. In the manner of Oriental potentates, he sat as judge in his own court and made a journey inland to settle a quarrel between two men as to which should be chief of a native tribe. His letters home give the unmistakable impression that Rajah Brooke was thoroughly enjoying himself.

He was aware that his title to Sarawak was shaky. All he had was an agreement signed by Rajah Muda which was yet to be endorsed by Sultan Omar Ali in Brunei. However, Brooke did not think it wise to go immediately to Brunei. He wanted to wait and let the sultan get used to the idea of having a white rajah governing his province before he approached Omar Ali about making the agreement with Rajah Muda permanent. When Brooke finally went, he found the famous city was nothing like the glamorous place he had imagined. Brunei city was as miserable looking as Brooke's own Kuching. It was a jumble of native-type houses built on stilts and joined with rattan bridges to keep people out of the mud that never seemed to dry. There were some permanent-type public buildings, but all were poorly kept.

Omar Ali proved to be a fat man with a child-like manner. He quickly agreed to legalize Brooke's rajahship of Sarawak and was pleased over the arrangement for him to receive an annual payment in lieu of the taxes that Brunei had never been able to collect anyway. Directly upon returning to Kuching, Brooke had to put down a revolt of Dayaks. This pleased Omar Ali. However, Brooke's next action pained the sultan, although Omar Ali could do nothing but smile and act pleased. This was Brooke's attack on the 20,000 or more pirates who swarmed around Borneo. The sultan had always received a cut of the pirates' booty in exchange for not disturbing their activity. This ended when Brooke suppressed piracy. After Brooke first fought a couple of sea battles with the pirates, most of the fighting was done by his good friend Captain Henry Keppel, who commanded a British Navy ship patrolling the Straits area. This help ended when Keppel was transferred to China. His successor, Captain Sir Edward Belcher, hated Borneo and Brooke. He saw no reason for helping the white rajah hold his private principality.

No one had expected Brooke to last long as Southeast Asia's only white rajah, but he got along quite well. In 1846 he persuaded the sultan to cede Lubuan Island, off the coast of Brunei, to the British. The British government then appointed Brooke Governor of Lubuan and British Consul-General to Brunei. The adventurous Englishman was now both a British government official and the independent ruler of his own state.

In this way Brooke laid the foundation for eventual British takeover in North Borneo, founding states that would someday take their place in the Federation of Malaysia. But quite a number of years, many fateful events, and two great wars had to come and go before this became possible.

CHAPTER SIX

The Growing Years

BRITISH policy in the second half of the nineteenth century still favored trade over territorial expansion. However, the government in London began to take more political interest in Southeast Asia as the British East India Company gradually collapsed. The decline began in 1833 when the company lost its China trade monopoly and new competitors took over some of its business. This forced the company to concentrate more on India, which worked to Singapore's disadvantage, since that port was founded primarily to assist the China trade. The disadvantage to Singapore was not in any loss of trade; in fact, business continued to grow. But because administration of the island was under the company's headquarters in faraway Calcutta, India, the East India Company administrators were not interested in improving Singapore or spending any money on it. So from 1850 on there was growing agitation by businessmen in Singapore to remove the island from Calcutta's control and to make the Straits Settlements (that is, all British interest states in Malaya) a Crown Colony under direct control of London.

As the shipping business continued to boom, farsighted men saw the need to develop native Malayan industries and resources. Little had been done in this line during the three hundred years that Europeans had been in Malaya. Settlements were still restricted to small river areas. These river-states, as they were called, were little more than *kampongs* or native Malay villages. The interior of the peninsula was still as wild as it had ever been. While sultans in the larger Malay states claimed suzerainty over these river-states, in actual practice they could exercise little control. The situation resembled the relationship between James Brooke and Omar Ali of Brunei: Brooke owed allegiance to Brunei, but Omar Ali was powerless to enforce his will on the White Rajah of Sarawak. Malacca and Penang held on as entrepôts, but had become of minor importance. Commercially speaking, Malaya was Singapore and Singapore was Malaya. The entire population of the Malay Peninsula at the midpoint of the nineteenth century was estimated at only 300,000.

Two factors of extreme importance to the peninsula's future were the development of the tin industry and the influx of a large number of Chinese immigrants. Both would play a decidedly important part in Malaya's future, and the two were tied together. The Chinese were imported by their fellow countrymen who developed large-scale tin mining in Perak and Sengalor states. Tin became so important that today the Malay Peninsula supplies the bulk of the world's tin supply. The mining is carried on in the plains area where the metal is extracted from alluvial sand that has been washed down from the mountains during a million years of erosion.

While development of the tin industry gave the Malay economy a much-needed local product boost, it introduced disturbing racial discord that has increased with the years and continues to the present. The seed of all current racial troubles in Malaysia goes back to the Chinese immigration of the mid-nineteenth century.

The trouble was and still is that the Chinese are extremely aggressive and brilliant businessmen. They soon dominate economically any area where they settle. In the tin mining areas the Chinese population soon equalled the Malayan population. Racial resentment arose inevitably as the Chinese prospered to a greater extent than the native people. There was an equal resentment on the part of the Chinese who, although they comprised half the population, were deprived of all political participation in the state. Religion also played its part in increasing racial discord. The Chinese were primarily Buddhist, whereas the Malays were Muslim.

The tin mining settlements were similar to the old Western towns of the United States. Gambling, lawlessness, and fighting were common and little could be done about it. Later the development of Chinese secret societies (on the order of the tongs of New York and San Francisco Chinatowns) added to the trouble. These societies were formed by immigrants banding together for mutual protection, but soon they were like private nations. Members were under the absolute orders of the society leaders who held court and even sentenced members to death for infraction of society rules. Each society was independent and often made war on other Chinese secret societies.

Tin had been mined in Malaya for nearly a thousand years before this time, since the metal was in demand to alloy with copper to produce bronze. This mining was small scale, however, and was carried on in a primitive fashion. A canal was cut beside a river which ran through an alluvial tin deposit. Ore-bearing sand was pushed into the canal. Water from the river was diverted through the canal, washing the sand away and leaving the heavier tin on the bottom of the canal. This is the principle of the sluice box which was used by the California gold miners in 1849.

The Chinese introduced an improved method of mining. First they dug holes in the earth to locate tin-bearing sand. This sand was dug out and carried in baskets on the backs of coolies to specially built sluice boxes where as much of the tin as possible was separated. Then women and children, using wooden pans called *dulangs,* panned the tailings to get the tin not caught in the sluice boxes. This double method greatly increased production. The Chinese miners had to pay a portion of their profit to the sultans for mining privileges. Thus tin rapidly became the mainstay of the sultans' treasuries.

An attempt to grow spices failed completely. Beginning with Stamford Raffles, numerous people tried planting nutmeg and clove trees, and at one time there was a spice boom. But those who invested in Malay spice plantations eventually lost everything, for the trees grew well at first and then sickened and died after a few years.

Promoters of Malay industry had better luck with gutta-percha, a rubberlike substance obtained from sap of the *getah* tree. The rubberish compound could be made to harden on exposure to air, but it could be softened in hot water so it could be molded into various shapes. Although unknown to Europeans in Malaya until the mid-1840s, gutta-percha had been used by Malays for centuries. Charles Buckley quotes an interesting article published in an 1856 issue of the Singapore *Free Press* which said that gutta-percha had been used since "time immemorial" by inland Malay tribes who molded it into handles for krisses and swords. "It was first brought to the attention of Europeans by a Malay of Singapore, who in the year 1842, commenced manufacturing riding whips of gutta. These had all the tough and elastic properties for which the *shamboks* [rhinoceros-hide whips of South Africa] are so celebrated."

The substance got its greatest boost in 1851 when a British experimenter discovered that gutta made a perfect insulation for submarine cables which were just coming into use for telegraph lines between England proper and its channel islands. In 1844 Singapore exported one and a half *piculs* of gutta. (A picul is an Asian measure which denotes the amount of weight a man can carry on his back. It varies from 132 to 140 pounds.) In four years this jumped to 21,600 pounds. The price began at eight dollars a picul in 1844 and by the end of the century reached a price of seven hundred dollars a picul. The discovery that it could be used for bicycle tires aided the boom.

It was not all work in Singapore in the mid-nineteenth century. This account from the *Free Press* shows how everyone, native and European, enjoyed the traditional holidays:

"New Year's Day was celebrated with the usual rejoicings, the Esplanade being crowded with the natives who had assembled to enjoy the accustomed sports and pastimes. There was an abundance of amusement suited for every taste, from a well-greased pole for those inclined to display their powers of perseverance to dancing girls for those fond of the ballet. There were three hack-pony races with a number of entries, foot races, and a pig race, or rather a race after a pig.

"The most exciting sport, however is football [soccer] in which all joined. The day was fine, a breeze for the most part prevailing, and the varied and gay costumes of the natives, and especially the Malays, who were present in great number and dressed in their best, formed altogether a very animated and enlivening scene, enhanced by the good humor which seemed to animate all.

"The aquatic sports were no less well got up and successful. There were sailing races, yachts, sampans and canoes, as well as rowing. All were well contested, and proved highly interesting."

Tigers were a problem at this time, with an average of one death per day attributed to the ferocious cats. Cats as a species hate water, but tigers can swim, and their increase on Singapore island was caused by the big cats swimming the Strait of Singapore between the island and Johore. The situation got so bad that the *Free Press* suggested several possible solutions. One was to import skilled tiger hunters from India. Another was to "employ third class convicts to beat the jungle once a month with tomtoms, horns, etc., which, if they do not lead to destruction of the tigers, may frighten them away from the island."

John Cameron also added stories about tigers in his book, *Our Tropical Possessions in Malayan India.* Cameron wrote that tiger hunting was difficult. "There is nothing exciting about tiger shooting here, and consequently few join it from pleasure ... It is usual to tie a bullock to a stake in the center of guarded trees as a lure. Watches of this kind often continue for weeks and the chances of a tiger appearing are ten to one." Even experts found the Singapore tigers too wily for them. Cameron told about an "old American backwoodsman, who has many years devoted himself to tiger destruction, but he has had but poor sport of it here in Singapore—though I believe he killed many tigers in Johore." This American was said to have been very eccentric but was much liked by both the Malays and the Europeans in Singapore.

The papers of the period carried a full share of crime news. Pirates were still active, and Chinese secret societies were more troublesome than ever. Catholicism had come to Southeast Asia with the Portuguese but had made few inroads against the strongly entrenched Muslim religion. There were scattered converts among the Chinese. Buckley reports: "A very slight pretense was laid hold of for sacking and pillaging the plantations belonging to Christian Chinese and for carrying off individuals and holding them for ransom." He claimed the kidnaping was done by one or more of the secret societies from whose ranks the converts had come. Leaders feared that such defections would destroy the societies. The *Free Press* said: "The Christians came to town from all parts of the country as to a place of refuge, and people yesterday in flourishing circumstances are today reduced to the greatest misery. The list of planters ruined proves there exists a conspiracy throughout the entire island."

The anti-religious attacks were not confined only to Chinese converts. The vengeful secret societies also attacked priests, as witness this story from the *Free Press:* "The Revd. Mr. Issaly had gone to Sungei Benoi to attend a sick Christian woman, wife of a Chinese planter. He was informed that a band of heathen Chinese intended to attack him. He took refuge in the jungle and stayed for twenty-four hours. He finally escaped to the coast where he met a boatman who charged him the exorbitant sum of eight dollars to carry him to town."

The police went to execute some arrest warrants for the destruction. They had arrested twelve men when they were attacked by a force of two hundred Chinese, acting on secret society orders to rescue their fellow members. A police gunboat was sent up the Singapore River to aid in the fight. It is rather startling to learn that this attacking force sent to restore order included thirty convicts from the Singapore jail. Although Singapore evidently trusted its own convicts, using them for public work and even as auxiliary police, the city did not appreciate "foreign" convicts. When Calcutta tried to use Malaya as a site for transporting Europeans convicted in the India courts, the entire city rose up in righteous wrath.

In the meantime, Sir James Brooke (he had recently been knighted) was having trouble in Sarawak with the Chinese, who resented river tolls instituted by Brooke as a tax on their gold mining in the interior. Suddenly a large Chinese force attacked Kuching. Brooke fled just in time to save his life, but returned with a superior force and defeated the rebels.

What Brooke did in his own Sarawak was none of Great Britain's business, but he was also governor of Lubuan Island which was a British government position. An angry Englishman who had been an agent for Brooke used this technicality to prefer charges against the white rajah in Singapore. He charged that Brooke had been unnecessarily cruel in putting down disturbances in the Lubuan territory. After an official hearing in Singapore, the charges against Brooke were dropped. However, the action hurt Brooke. Borneo natives took it as a sign that the white rajah no longer enjoyed the confidence and respect of the British government. Brooke made no effort to change his ways. He continued to enlarge his state of Sarawak at the expense of Brunei. The weak Brunei sultan could do nothing about it.

Brooke was ailing and it was expected that his illegitimate son would succeed him. This son was a surprise to everyone. He turned up late in Brooke's life, claiming he was the result of an affair Brooke had while back in England. Brooke did not question the young man's story and accepted him as his son. However, the young man—whose name was Reuben George—did not live up to his father's expectations. Brooke did not feel that he had the ability to be a future ruler of Sarawak. So before he died of a paralytic stroke in June 1868, James Brooke made a will leaving Sarawak to his nephew, Charles Johnson, with the understanding that Charles would provide an annuity for Brooke's son. Charles changed his name to Charles Brooke and became the second White Rajah of Sarawak.

Charles Brooke also tried to enlarge Sarawak, but he ran into competition in North Borneo. There, an American named Torrey secured trading rights which he then sold to Baron Von Overbeck of Austria and Alfred Dent of England. Then in 1877 Von Overbeck and Dent persuaded the sultan to cede them the entire section of North Borneo which would eventually become the Malaysian state of Sabah. There was a conflict in that the Sultan of the Island of Sulu also claimed the territory. Sulu had once been a vassal of Brunei, but he had broken away to form a new sultanate when Brunei's power waned. Just to be on the safe side, since Sulu's military power was greater than Brunei's, Von Overbeck made a separate treaty with the Sultan of Sulu in which the sultan ceded the two traders the same land that they had obtained from Brunei. Von Overbeck later withdrew from the partnership, and Dent, together with other business associates,

The Growing Years

formed the British North Borneo Chartered Company to administer the 30,000 square miles they had obtained.

These imperial land grabs did not please the British government. One official complained that if something was not done soon to curb Brooke and the North Borneo Company, nothing would be left of Brunei.

However, change was in the wind. Soon the British government was forced to alter its policy of not taking over local governments. This policy, it will be remembered, was based not on humanitarian desires to protect these native governments, but on a reluctance of the British government to take on additional expensive administrative responsibilities such as it had in India.

In Borneo the Dutch were claiming larger sections of land. Germany was also showing interest in Borneo, and the actions of the American Torrey indicated a possible interest of the United States. Under the circumstances the British government thought it wise to grant the North Borneo Company a royal charter.

Meanwhile conditions on the Malay Peninsula were worsening. Several states were in civil war. Secret society fights were disrupting tin mining. Piracy was on the increase. And lawlessness in some areas reached the point of near anarchy. As early as 1873 a group of 250 Singapore merchants petitioned Governor Ord of the Straits Settlement to do something about the disorder "for the richest areas of the peninsula have fallen into the hands of lawless persons." Governor Ord forwarded the petition to London where it was considered for some time. Nothing was done until a new governor was appointed. He was Colonel Andrew Clarke, who received these instructions: "The anarchy which prevails and appears to be increasing in parts of the peninsula, and the consequent injury to trade and British interests generally, render it necessary to consider seriously whether any step can be taken to improve this condition.

"Her Majesty's government have, it need hardly be said, no desire to interfere in the internal affairs of the Malay States. But looking to the well-being of the British Settlements, Her Majesty's government find it incumbent upon them to employ such influence as they possess with the native princes to rescue, if possible, those fertile and productive countries from ruin."

Clarke's instruction went on to order him to make an investigation to see whether it was advisable to appoint a British resident commission to each state. The instructions hastened to add that a Resident (actually an overseer of the sultan) would be appointed only with the "full consent of the Native Government."

Colonel Clarke, the new governor of the Straits Settlements, did not need to make an investigation as suggested in his orders. He had already decided that British intervention was necessary. He obtained the services of W. A. Pickering, a man who had had much experience with the Chinese through several years in Taiwan. He sent Pickering into Perak state, where Chinese secret societies were causing trouble in the tin-mining area. Pickering arranged for leaders of the two factions to meet with Clarke at Pangkor Island at the mouth of the Perak River in January 1874. Leaders of the rival Chinese groups, the Ghee Hin Society and the Hai San Society, were told in no uncertain terms that peace was necessary and that they would be fined $50,000 each if the peace was broken. Clarke divided the tin territory, giving an exclusive territory to each society. He also settled an argument among the Malays concerning who would succeed to the Perak throne. He then arranged for the new ruler, Sultan Abdullah, to accept a British Resident whose counsel was required for all matters except those involving the Malays' religion and racial customs.

The matter of British protection of Perak settled, Clarke next intervened in Sengalor. This state had been disrupted for some time by civil war, and the disturbance led to an increase in piracy along Sengalor's coast which fronts on the Straits of Malacca. Clarke demanded that the pirates be punished and had a British naval squadron anchored off the coast. The sultan took the hint. The suspected pirates were tried and hanged. (Sir Frank Swettenham, then a young governmental official, said years later that the wrong men were hanged. This did not bother Clarke, since the action frightened both guilty and innocent and worked toward keeping future peace.)

In his report to London, Colonel (later Sir) Andrew Clarke claimed that he had not forced a Resident upon Perak but had merely served as the chairman for a meeting of the Malays who

The Growing Years

made the decision. When Clarke first went to Perak, the sultan had in his employ a British adventurer known as "Captain Speedy" who served as the sultan's chief of police. Clarke left Captain Speedy as acting Resident until September 1874 when young Frank Swettenham was appointed Assistant Resident until a Resident could be appointed from London.

Swettenham would in time make quite a name for himself in Malaya and even leave his name on the land in the form of Port Swettenham in Sengalor. He was a great admirer of the Malay people and wrote some very popular books, including *Malay Sketches,* and an autobiography, *Footprints in Malaya.* In one of his *Malay Sketches,* Swettenham gives an idea of the worth placed on young colonials just fresh from England: "So in January 1871, at the age of twenty, I found myself where I would be [i.e. in Malaya] . . . The Government of the Colony paid me the dollar equivalent of £240 a year, and added that, if that was not sufficient for my needs, I should look to my relatives for help during the next two years during which I should be learning my trade and be of no particular use to my employers."

However, young Swettenham became very proficient in the Malay language, proving more useful than the usual beginner in colonial service. His linguistic ability got him the job of interpreting for top officials and brought him to the notice of those who could advance the young man's career. It also nearly got him killed in the first revolt against the Residency system.

Four Residencies were established in Malaya. In every case they were at first welcomed by the Malay ruler, for it meant British help against enemies threatening to unseat him. However, this initial welcome disappeared when it quickly became apparent that the British had come to rule, not to help. The Residents considered themselves as the rulers of their Residencies and the sultans as their messenger boys.

The first break came in Perak state. When the British first moved in, Captain Speedy was appointed acting Resident with Frank Swettenham as his assistant. Soon Speedy was replaced by James Birch, a colonial official from Singapore. Swettenham was returned to interpreter duties and Speedy was made Assistant Resident. Birch immediately destroyed all the goodwill that Speedy and Swettenham had built up. He stunned the sultan by announcing that he would collect all the taxes hereafter and would give the sultan what he needed to run his court. Next Birch announced that all female slaves would have to be liberated, that putting people into slavery for non-payment of debt must be abolished, and that Christian ethics would be observed.

The infuriated sultan was goaded still further by Major General Sir W. F. D. Jervois, the newly appointed Governor of the Straits Settlements. Jervois was convinced that none of the Malay sultans and rajahs was fit to rule. He reported to London that the Residency system, based on advising local princes only, would not work. "My proposal," he wrote, "is to govern the countries in the name of the sultans by means of Queen's Commissioners." London officials gave serious study to Jervois's proposal because they had evidence of Germany's interest in Malaya and greatly feared that some foreign nation would attempt to get a foothold in the British sphere of influence in Southeast Asia.

Meanwhile, Malay resentment of Birch and the British in Perak reached the exploding point. Neither Birch nor Jervois showed much concern for the Malay resentment. Reports reached Birch that he had been marked for death. He shrugged and said, "If they kill Mr. Birch, then ten other Mr. Birchs will come to take his place."

He was wrong only in the number. When Birch was finally slain, it was not ten but 1,200 "Mr. Birches" who came to avenge his death.

CHAPTER SEVEN

The Residents of Malaya

THE conquest of India and the beginning of the conquest of Burma were made by the East India Company. The British government itself was not directly involved. In the same manner the conquest of Malaya, beginning with Raffles and extending through the formation of the Federation of Malaya, was effected by imperialistic individuals over the objections and nervousness of the British government back home which did not want to provoke a foreign war. The conquests of the Brooke rajahs in Borneo pushed into territory which the Dutch claimed. Siam claimed several of the northern Malay States. France had carved out her sphere of influence in Indochina. And the Germans, who had taken Samoa, were hungrily eying the Malay Peninsula.

These foreign interests in Malaya and Southeast Asia made British officials and merchants on the scene in Singapore more certain than ever that Great Britain should assert her rights in the area. They kept pushing forward, seizing every excuse to act and then apologetically informing Whitehall—the British Foreign Office in London—that they had been "forced by circumstances" to do so.

Governor Jervois candidly made known his feelings. The sultans and rajahs must be reduced to figureheads taking orders from British Residents. Birch in Perak was strongly pushing just this policy. Sultan Abdullah at first refused to go along with Birch's orders. When the Resident threatened to bring in British troops, the sultan reluctantly signed the proclamation demanded by Birch, establishing tax collectors under British control and abolishing slavery-for-debt. Then under Birch's continued pressure Abdullah agreed to cede Perak to the British for a pension of $2,000 a month.

This agreement was concluded on October 1, 1875. Two weeks later Abdullah called a secret meeting of his highest officials. They agreed to murder Birch while he and Frank Swettenham were on a trip to the interior to post proclamations declaring Great Britain's intention to govern the state. On November 1 Birch's houseboat arrived at Pasir Salak on the Perak River. Rajah Lela of Pasir Salik had already received a gift of a jeweled *kris* (dagger) from Sultan Abdullah. This was a secret order for the rajah to kill Birch.

Lela gave the order and a soldier named Pandak Indut carried it out, thrusting a spear through the rattan wall of the floating bathhouse attached to the back of Birch's boat. Then another Malay rushed in and hacked the wounded Englishman's body with a sword. Frank Swettenham had taken another route and escaped his assassins.

Two days later word of Birch's murder reached Singapore. Governor Jervois rushed to Perak with a force of 150 men and urgently requested additional troops from India. He feared the assassination would trigger a general uprising against the British. Twelve hundred troops were sent from Calcutta, and Jervois occupied Perak state for the next eighteen months. All those implicated in Birch's assassination were relentlessly hunted down. Rajah Lela and four others were hanged. Sultan Abdullah and several others were exiled. A rajah named Yusuf was made regent after it was determined that he had had no part in the murder.

The trouble was scarcely settled in Perak when a new disturbance broke out in the state of Sungei Ujong. Jervois sent in six hundred soldiers to restore order. Then in November 1876 Jervois half-persuaded, half-forced the rulers of a number of small central states to form a federation which eventually became the present Malay state of Negri Sembilan. The state of Johore, across the strait from Singapore, was already under strong

The Residents of Malaya   61

British domination. Jervois's actions gave Great Britain effective political control of all the peninsula except the states of Kedah, Kelantan, and Trengganu which were still claimed by the Siamese.

All the Residents who have left memoirs have been unanimous in agreeing that theirs was the world's worst job. The British government refused to go along with the requests of both Clarke and his successor Jervois to take over the Malay states completely. Orders directly from London forbade interference in the internal affairs of any Malay state by the assigned Resident. Cooperation, London insisted, must be accomplished by persuasion and advice. Unfortunately for the Residents, the sultans and rajahs did not want to be persuaded or advised.

The unenviable job of taking over as Resident in Perak was assumed by Sir Hugh Low, who had been an administrative officer on the Borneo island of Lubuan for the previous thirty years. Low, according to historian Harry Miller, was "one of the greatest Residents in the history of the peninsula. He laid a pattern which others were to follow elsewhere in the peninsula . . . He had learned how to adapt the administrative ways of the West to people whose existence had been ruled by custom and religion. Low soon won trust by his sympathetic approach and by clearly showing his earnest wish to establish good relations and not to interfere with Malay customs."

Frank Swettenham in Sengalor state was another who understood the advantage of getting along with the sultans rather than trying to use force as Birch had done. Where Birch tried to eradicate Malay customs, Swettenham studied them and respected them. Instead of laughing at Malay creation legends or condemning them, Swettenham found them interesting, and much of his writing for publication dealt with legends of the Malays. One story he retold explained how the spirits were created. The Creator fashioned the first man of clay and put a spirit in the head of the clay image. The spirit was so strong that it burst the clay body. The pieces flew in all directions to create the spirits of the air, land, and water who bedeviled or helped the common man. The Creator then tried again. This time He mixed iron with the clay and made a body strong enough to contain the spirit of life. Thus was the first man created.

John Cameron of the *Straits Times* in Singapore was another who helped the British understand the Malays by publishing folklore and stories of Malay culture and customs. Cameron was particularly interested in the aborigine tribes. "These tribes," he wrote, "wander about the hills and valleys very much as they did in olden times but with this difference, that they have now altogether forsaken the coast line, and retreated to the fastnesses of the interior before the encroaching inroads of the Malays. The more lonely the spot of their encampment the better suited to their tastes. It is difficult to conjecture as to their numbers, but it is generally believed that they do not exceed 7,000 or 8,000 souls."

Cameron records several creation myths of these aborigines. A curious fact is that most of them claim that their forefathers came to the Malay Peninsula in boats, hinting that the myths might be distorted ancestral memories of a prehistoric migration. In one of these the tribe claimed their ancestors came from Heaven in a boat which sailed around and around the world until it finally became grounded on a high mountain that extended up from the sea. The mariners multiplied until attacked by enemies. Then a great hero named Batin Alam built an ark and carried all his people away to Malaya where they have lived ever since.

Batin was also given as the name of the Adam of another aborigine tribe. This Batin was created by God in Heaven. God thought Batin so beautiful that He wanted his creation duplicated. So God sent Batin and a woman companion in a boat to earth, and from these two all the people of the tribe descended. Since it is improper for brother to mate with a sister, the legend insists that the children of Batin's wife were born in her legs, one in each leg, and therefore were not brother and sister.

Still another legend of these tribes points to a creation that is much like what scientists believe. As quoted by Cameron: "The ground, they say, on which we stand is not solid. It is but the skin of the earth. In ancient times God broke up this skin, so the world was destroyed and overwhelmed by water."

Then a mountain appeared above the water and a covered boat floated to a stop against the upraised land. Inside the boat were a man and woman which God had made and set adrift.

Most folklore deals with the olden days of a people, but Cameron repeats a legend he got from a Catholic priest who was a missionary to an aborigine tribe near Malacca. This unique tale concerns the tribe's prediction of the end of the world: "A great wind will rise accompanied by rain. The waters will descend with rapidity. Lightning will fill all the spaces around, and the mountains will sink down. Then a great heat will occur. There will be no more night and the earth will wither like the grass in the field. God will then come down surrounded by an immense whirlwind of flame."

Then, after the people are judged, their souls will be burned and weighed. Those who come through the fire purified will go to heaven. The rest will be condemned to hell where they will be punished by serpents and tigers. And then "lastly, God having taken a light from hell, will close the portals and then set fire to the earth."

Sir Frank Swettenham gave his own reasons for studying Malay myths, superstitions, and legends in one of his *Malay Sketches*. He began by saying that many said it is impossible for the Western mind to understand the character of the Easterner. He disagreed. "If you live in the East for years—if you make yourself perfectly familiar with the language, literature, customs, prejudices, and superstitions of the people; if you lie on the same floor with them, eat out of the same dish, fight with them and against them, join them in their sorrows and their joys—then reading their character is no longer an impossible task."

John Coleman, another *Straits Times* reporter, wrote a description of a Malay village of this period. Things in the back country are so little changed that his 110-year-old account might well have been written today:

"Their hamlets are composed of twenty or thirty neat little houses or huts. They are built of leaves of a species of palm tree, usually raised on posts some four or five feet from the ground, with little ladders reaching up to the doorways. The houses are uniform in appearance, but not planted with much regard to order. The entire hamlet generally reposes under the shadow of a cluster of coconuts and other fruit trees. The people of a hamlet are generally connected by birth or by marriage, and share each other's joys and sorrows."

All these early writers spoke with admiration of the Malays' honesty. Piracy was not regarded by them as dishonest, but as a profession. In fact many of the pirates operated under orders of their sultans. All, except Malays of the ruling classes, obeyed their leaders without question. The Residents learned early that there would never be any trouble with the Malays if the sultans and rajahs could be controlled.

"In their domestic relations they are frank, amiable, and often generous," Coleman wrote. "Deceit forms but a small part of their nature. They are strongly attached to home and family."

Women had much more freedom in Malaya than in any other part of the East, or for that matter than either American or European women of the time. This freedom was surprising when one considers that the Malays were devout—but not fanatical—Muslims. They practiced polygamy and were permitted four wives by the Koran. Apparently few Malay men took advantage of this religious law. Coleman wrote, "I once asked a sensible Malay how it came that so few of his countrymen had more than one wife, when the Prophet [Mohammed] authorized polygamy both by precept and by example.

"He replied, 'The women in the Prophet's time must have been different from what they are now; for I never knew a man yet who kept two wives in one house here and led a happy life.'"

The outstanding contribution of the four British Residents in the years before 1900—in addition to keeping order—was their vigorous support of resource development. They laid the beginning of a system of roads which has developed today into the best in the Orient. Then in 1885 Sir Hugh Low in Perak state built a railroad from the tin mines to the coast. Shortly after this Sir Frank Swettenham began work on a railroad in Sengalor state. Despite the poor soil, the Residents expanded agriculture to meet increased demands caused by the steady influx of Chinese and Indians. Pineapples were grown successfully in Johore, sugar plantations were started, and tapioca growing became commercially important. Copra and palm oil became important products. Coffee, however, was a failure. As with the spice cultivation, when coffee trees were first planted they grew well and there was a rush of European investors to cash in on the new crop. However, the climate was unsuited to the trees. Soon they died and investors suffered heavy losses.

The failing coffee plantations were replaced by rubber plantations which in time would develop into an industry second only to trade and tin as the economic backbone of the Malay Peninsula. Natural rubber is a product of the Americas and was not introduced into Malaya until 1876. At that time plantation owners had not yet learned that coffee trees were unsuited for the peninsula and only a few experimented with rubber. One of these was Resident Sir Hugh Low in Perak. Then, when coffee failed, a larger number planted rubber trees.

Early explorers found the Indians of Central and South America using crude rubber, but the discovery made little impact until 1735 when a French explorer took samples back to France. He called the substance *caoutchouc* after the Indian name for the tree from which the rubber juice—latex—is taken. Then in 1823 Charles Macintosh, a Scottish inventor, produced the Macintosh raincoat by putting a thin layer of latex between two layers of cloth. By this time *caoutchouc* had been named "rubber" by Joseph Priestly, a British chemist, who discovered that it could rub out pencil writing. At this time rubber products were sticky in hot weather and became so hard in cold weather that they often cracked. This slowed the development of the rubber industry until the American Charles Goodyear accidentally discovered a way to cure latex with a heat process so that the product stayed firm in both heat and cold.

Goodyear's discovery spurred the rubber industry. As a result the British government imported 70,000 seeds, part of which were planted in greenhouses in Kew Gardens, London. The rest were sent to Malaya and Ceylon.

The demands for rubber increased as new products were developed. By 1890 there were 50,000 acres of rubber trees in Malaya and Ceylon. Then the invention of the automobile brought a demand for rubber tires. This demand was so great that by 1905 the number of acres in rubber plantations in Malaya and Ceylon doubled. By 1910 when the rubber boom was at its height, Malaya, Ceylon, Borneo, and Indonesia were producing the greater part of the world's export supply of rubber.

The growth of rubber's importance and the realization that

A Tamil Indian boy checks the late flow from a rubber tree in a Malaysian plantation. The rubber industry once provided the country's second most important export product after tin, but it has been hard hit by competition from synthetic rubber. The government is encouraging rubber growers to switch to palm oil, for which there is greater demand.

rubber trees would flourish in Malaya's poor soil caused a greater interest among British government officials in tightening their control over Malaya. This led to two important developments. One was the formation of the Federation of Malaya. The other was the ridding of Siamese control in several of the northern Malay states, establishing the present northern border of Malaysia.

The Federation of Malaya grew from an idea of Sir Frank Swettenham who recommended in 1893 that the four Malay states having British Residents be formed into a federation with a central government. This would include Perak, Sengalor, Pahang, and Negri Sembilan. In his recommendation to the British Colonial Office in London, Swettenham pointed out that communications were so difficult in Malaya that Singapore had no really effective control of the Residents in the four states. Each did very much as he pleased. If a Federation was formed with a Resident-General, this official would be able to oversee the actions of each Resident. The Resident-General would in turn be directly responsible to the High Commissioner for the Straits Settlements or to the Governor of Singapore. The Resident-General and the central Federation would not make laws but would ensure that the same laws were passed in each state so there would be uniformity in taxation and governmental policies.

The Colonial Office agreed to the Federation, provided the sultans of the states found it acceptable. Inasmuch as the sultans had just about lost all their power to the Resident anyway, they did not see how the Federation would hurt their situation. While the Residents were supposed merely to advise and persuade, they were supported by both the British Fleet and the British Army. Commanders were easily persuaded to come to the aid of the Residents if necessary. A good reason for intervening could always be thought up to pacify the Colonial Office.

The Federation was formed July 1, 1896, with Sir Frank Swettenham as the first Resident-General. Swettenham was highly regarded, but the sultans quickly found that they were all reduced to the practical rank of rajah and that the Resident-General was the real sultan.

From the middle of the nineteenth century France had been gradually taking control of the Indochinese peninsula. The land that is now North and South Vietnam, Laos, and Cambodia came under French control. Then the French began nibbling away at Siam's eastern border. Great Britain was fearful of sharing a common border in Asia with the French, for it was sure to lead to trouble. The British began to support the Siamese in order to keep a free buffer state between Burma, which Great Britain controlled, and Laos and Cambodia which were in the hands of the French.

Both King Chulalongkorn of Siam and his late father, King Mongkut, feared the British. But most of Asia was falling to European imperialists during the nineteenth century, and Siam needed to play England against France in order to keep her independence. In 1902 an Anglo-Siamese treaty recognized Siam's paramount rights in the Malay states of Kelantan and Trengganu. However, Britain feared that France would move into these Siamese-controlled states and decided to bring them under British protection.

British historians claim that Siam agreed in a friendly manner to relinquish control of Kelantan, Trengganu, Kedah, and Perlis to Great Britain in exchange for certain concessions. In actuality, Siam was forced into the agreement. Siamese history records that King Chulalongkorn was so disturbed by what he considered British aggression that he became physically ill. Great Britain by the agreement did not gain total control of the four Malay states, but only the right to afford "protection." Swettenham by this time had risen to the position of High Commissioner of the Straits Settlement, the top British government position in Southeast Asia. He tried to get the sultans of Kelantan, Trengganu, Kedah, and Perlis to join the Federation of Malaya. They resisted the suggestion vigorously, and Swettenham did not care to use force. These states became known as the Unfederated States of Malaya, and their sultans had more internal control than did the rulers of the Federated States of Malaya.

Conditions as a whole were improving in Malaya because of the Residents who worked hard to improve sanitary conditions and build industry. Tin production rose until half the world's supply came from the Malay Peninsula. Iron mines were opened in Johore. Chinese and Indians continued to immigrate to Malaya in great numbers. The population increased enormously. This was partly because of immigration and partly because of decreased infant mortality, resulting from better health standards introduced by the Residents.

The entrepôt trade in Singapore continued to grow as part of a world-wide distribution system. For example, American cotton was shipped to India, where it was woven into cloth, and then transported to Singapore for further distribution in China, Indochina, and Indonesia. American cotton had long been an important trade item in Singapore and was one of the reasons why officials took such a calm view of the *Alabama* affair in 1865.

The *Alabama* was a famous Confederate raider which attacked Yankee shipping in the Far East. British sympathy was with the American South in the Civil War, and the *Alabama* was welcomed in Singapore harbor after sinking three United States ships in Sunda Straits. John Coleman reported that the *Alabama*'s captain, Semmes, was told that the Yankees had just burned Charleston, South Carolina. "It is no matter," Semmes replied, pointing to the Confederate ensign on his ship's mast. "That flag will never come down."

After coaling at Singapore, the *Alabama* sailed northward along the west coast of the Malay Peninsula where she took a merchant vessel, *Martaban*. The *Martaban*'s captain angrily claimed to be British and produced the ship's papers to show that she was of British registry. The crew and captain, however, were American. The ship had been registered in India to sail under the British flag as a subterfuge to outwit Confederate raiders. Knowing this, Semmes sank the ship and landed the crew on the Malayan coast after extracting a signed promise not to bear arms against the Confederacy for the rest of the war.

The *Martaban*'s captain registered a vigorous complaint to British authorities. There was no question about it. The ship was flying the British flag and was legitimately registered to sail under British authority. Although Semmes did not return to Singapore, he dispatched a letter which was printed in the *Straits Times* three days after the sinking. The Confederate captain maintained that his action was justified and that, British flag or no British flag, the ship was a Yankee vessel. Since all the influential people of Singapore liked Semmes and had Confederate leanings, the matter was dropped. Coleman claimed that the *Alabama* was so feared that twelve Yankee vessels refused to leave Singapore harbor while Semmes was in the vicinity.

CHAPTER EIGHT

The Fall of Singapore

ALTHOUGH the sultans chafed under the restraints put on them by the Residents, the first two decades of the twentieth century were good years for Malaya. The '30s were bad years because world trade was suppressed by the worldwide depression that followed the stock market crash in the United States in 1929. Things began to improve in the mid-1930s when the growth of Nazism in Germany caused Great Britain to start rearming. The outbreak of World War II in Europe in September 1939 definitely caused business to boom, but it also raised some apprehensions as to the future of Singapore.

Singapore did not fear the Germans. They were too far away and Hitler's naval threat was primarily the submarine. There was doubt in Singapore that the submarine threat would affect the Southeast Asia area much. It was too far from German bases.

However, the Japanese threat was real indeed. Japan had been fighting China in Manchuria since 1931 and had been at all-out war with China since 1937. Japan had concluded treaties with both Hitler's Germany and Mussolini's Italy. She was in possession of Canton, just up the Pearl River from Britain's Hong Kong, and the island of Hainan which put her in striking distance of Southeast Asia. After the collapse of France in 1940, Japan moved into French Indochina and concluded a non-

The Fall of Singapore

aggression pact with Thailand (Siam) which permitted Japanese troops to cross Thai territory.

These were all ominous signs, but still there was only mild worry in Singapore. The official position was that although Japan would probably attack somewhere in Southeast Asia, the attack would be aimed at Dutch oil fields in Borneo. Singapore, both the citizens and the British Army felt, was "impregnable." The term "Gibraltar of the East" was freely used in discussing the military position of the British base in Malaya. However, reinforcements were sent to strengthen the Army forces there. All the new soldiers were pitifully untrained, as future events were to show. This could not be helped. The British had suffered a near-disastrous defeat on the European continent and narrowly escaped total rout by a brilliantly conducted evacuation at Dunkirk. England was enduring an all-out air blitz as Hitler tried to soften up the island for a coming invasion. The best troops from Australia, Canada, and India were already fighting in Europe. There were none left to reinforce Singapore.

Winston Churchill, the British Prime Minister, did dispatch a battleship, *Prince of Wales,* the battlecruiser *Repulse,* and four destroyers to the Singapore area. He thought this show of naval force, plus the threat of the United States Pacific Fleet based at Pearl Harbor in the Hawaiian Islands, would deter any Japanese attempt to make an amphibious landing in British territory in the Far East.

President Franklin D. Roosevelt had frozen Japanese assets in the United States when Japan announced its "protectorate" over Indochina. This cut off Japan's access to imports from the United States. War now seemed inevitable between the United States and Japan. However, Japan sent a peace mission to Washington for last-minute negotiations which accomplished nothing.

The question of further bolstering British defenses in Malaya was discussed by the United Kingdom Chiefs of Staff. Prime Minister Churchill did not think reinforcements necessary. As he recorded in his book, *The War Against Japan:* "The political situation in the Far East does not seem to require, and the strength of our Air Force by no means warrants, the maintenance of such large forces in the Far East at this time."

In the meantime Japan kept pouring more troops into Indochina. An official Japanese government statement placed the number of Japanese soldiers in Indochina at 50,000. Actually it was 200,000. This discrepancy in numbers seems to have escaped the notice of United States and British intelligence officers. The announced 50,000 troops could possibly be needed to "preserve order in Indochina because of troubles arising from the fall of France," as the Japanese announced. But 200,000 troops could only mean that a new aggressive campaign was being planned for some Southeast Asian target. The Japanese were then fighting a bitter war with Chiang Kai-shek in central China and could not possibly have spared so many men just for a police action to prevent a local war between Vietnam and Thailand, as they claimed.

The British still based their plans on the impregnability of Singapore. With 85,000 British troops in Malaya, backed by the battleship *Prince of Wales* and the cruiser *Repulse,* there was supreme confidence in London that Malaya was not in any immediate danger. Commanders in Malaya were asking for reinforcements, but their requests were ignored.

A Japanese Foreign Office statement in November 1941 again rattled the sword. Ever since her attack on China, Japan had been plugging a "Co-Prosperity Sphere" in the Far East. This plan envisioned economic cooperation of Far East countries under Japanese domination. The statement, in the *Nippon Times,* an official government-dominated newspaper published in Tokyo, said: "Japan's Co-Prosperity Sphere must be acknowledged and Manchukuo [Japan's new name for Manchuria], China, Indochina, Thailand [Siam], the Netherlands East Indies and other states and protectorates must be allowed to establish their own political and economic relations with Japan without any interference of any kind."

This was a clear statement that Western nations would be shut completely out of the entire Far East area where Japan intended to be the dominant power. The warning had little diplomatic effect in London and Washington. The U.S. Secretary of State, Cordell Hull, continued to meet with Japanese Ambassador Kichisaburo Nomura with each side presenting its latest demands. While these fruitless Washington talks continued, a Japanese carrier fleet was already steaming toward Pearl Harbor where the American Pacific Fleet was based.

The Fall of Singapore

Winston Churchill was correct in his previous estimate that British ships in Southeast Asia operating from the great naval base in Singapore and the American Pacific Fleet operating out of Hawaii would pose a major threat to Japan's war aims. What he did not realize was that Japan had made careful plans to remove these threats before striking to bring about the Co-Prosperity Sphere which Japanese government-controlled newspapers had announced as inevitable.

On December 5 two Japanese convoys were spotted, but British intelligence thought they were mounting an attack on Siam. A general alert was declared in Singapore, but nothing else was done. Then two days later on December 7, 1941, the Japanese carrier fleet under Admiral Chuichi Nagumo struck a devastating blow at the American Fleet in Pearl Harbor. It was already December 8 in Singapore because of the International Date Line. Somewhere around midnight word flashed to Singapore that a Japanese amphibious landing was in progress at Kota Bahru in Kelantan on the east coast of Malaya. Japanese planes were also reported to be bombing strategic points in North Malaya. An hour later air raid sirens were screaming in Singapore.

There was surprise in Singapore but no panic. Residents and military alike were convinced that their military bastion was impregnable. Then word was received that the United States Fleet at Pearl Harbor had been knocked out by the Japanese attack. Shortly after this, news from the Philippine Islands indicated that the bulk of United States war planes there had been destroyed by the Japanese attack. British Malayan troops had not been able to prevent the Japanese landing at Kota Bahru. Soon a three-pronged attack was moving down the peninsula toward Singapore.

When the attack came the fleet was in Singapore harbor, but on the evening of December 8 it was dispatched northward to help defend the coast against further Japanese landings. The fleet, it will be remembered, consisted of *Prince of Wales, Repulse,* and the four destroyers. A report came in that a Japanese landing force had attacked Singora in Siam, about 180 miles north of Kota Bahru. This proved incorrect, and the fleet turned back in time to receive another message that the Japanese were landing at Kuantan, 150 miles south of Kota Bahru. The fleet then changed course and headed for Kuantan on the evening of December 9. Japanese planes were sighted on the morning of the 10th, but the battle did not begin until just after 11 A.M. when the first wave of Japanese bombers hit *Repulse*. The second wave of Japanese bombers attacked the battleship *Prince of Wales*, coming in at 1,000-foot altitude. Both of the *Prince of Wales*'s port propellers were knocked out and the steering gear so badly damaged that it was useless. The battleship could do nothing but flounder helplessly before the continued Japanese attacks.

Another torpedo-bomber attack sank *Repulse*. One of the destroyers came in and picked up eight hundred of the ship's thirteen hundred crewmen. An hour later *Prince of Wales* sank. Again the Japanese stood back and did not interfere when a British destroyer picked up survivors.

Loss of the two ships destroyed the backbone of British naval defense in Southeast Asia. For the first time, Singapore was stunned. So was London. Writing in his war memoirs years later, Prime Minister Churchill related how he was awakened in the night and informed of the loss. He said that in all the war he never received a greater shock. "There were no British or American capital ships . . . in the Pacific except the American survivors of Pearl Harbor, who were hastening back to California. Over all this vast expanse of waters Japan was supreme, and we everywhere were weak and naked."

On land the Japanese Army was also moving forward triumphantly. By New Year's Day, 1942, it had pushed the British back to Johore.

Some reinforcements landed, but they were poorly trained Indian troops. Other reinforcements started to Malaya, but were diverted as the situation grew worse on the peninsula. Churchill decided that the fall of Singapore was inevitable and that it was more important to keep open the Burma Road so that supplies could be funneled into China, where Chiang Kai-shek's army was fighting the Japanese on the Chinese mainland. Not wishing to lose both Burma and Singapore, the Prime Minister decided that if Singapore could be held "only for a few weeks, it is certainly not worth losing all our reinforcements and aircraft."

The decision infuriated the Australian government, for it left

The Fall of Singapore

Australia undefended and directly in the route of the advancing Japanese Army. The cream of Australia's fighting men were in Europe, and the Australians believed that the decision to concentrate British strength in Burma could possibly be fatal to them. This decision sealed Singapore's fate, although the fight would continue for another two and a half weeks. By the end of January 1942, the military situation on the Malay Peninsula was hopeless. On the night of January 30 the British forces began evacuating to Singapore Island, moving across the causeway that linked the island with the peninsula.

Singapore was in a desperate situation. Before the war the city had a half-million population. The retreating army and the accompanying flood of refugees swelled the population to more than a million. Each day the situation was made worse by continuous Japanese bombing. Ten thousand injured (both military and civilian bombing victims) jammed the hospitals. Food was still available, but water became a major problem. The pipeline that supplied water from Johore was destroyed by the Japanese, cutting off half the island's supply. The three reservoirs which supplied the remainder were under constant air and land bombardment.

The assault on Singapore itself began in earnest on the night of February 8, 1942. Sir Archibald Wavell, commander-in-chief of Far East British Army forces, flew in from his headquarters in Java. He quickly realized the hopelessness of the situation. Before leaving, Wavell ordered the remaining units of the air force to leave the island, but told the local commander, Lieutenant General A. E. Percival, that no surrender was contemplated and that Singapore's defenders must fight to the end. At the same time Churchill told the House of Commons in London that the defenders of Singapore numbered one hundred thousand. "In these circumstances the defenders must greatly outnumber Japanese forces who have crossed the Straits [i.e., those actually fighting on Singapore Island]. In a well-contested battle they should destroy them. At this stage there must be no thought of saving the troops or sparing the population. The battle must be fought to the bitter end," Churchill said.

Despite this show of defiance, the end was just a few days away. On February 11 some nurses, women, and civilians were evacuated on a cargo ship. One evacuation ship, *Vyner Brooke*, was torpedoed with a loss of three hundred women and children. Small boats and crafts were commandeered to take more refugees to Java and the Indonesian islands.

The city was ablaze. Death and destruction were everywhere. The soldiers were exhausted. Supplies were running low. General Percival informed General Wavell in Java that he doubted the city could hold out more than two more days. Wavell cabled: FULLY APPRECIATE YOUR SITUATION, BUT CONTINUED ACTION IS NECESSARY. Another group tried to escape the beleaguered island in fifty small boats. Forty of the boats were sunk by the Japanese.

By this time, Singapore city was one mass of devastation. The streets were impassable, and uncontrolled fires continued to burn. Still, orders from Java and London demanded that the defeated city keep fighting. Finally on the morning of February 14—St. Valentine's Day—General Percival was informed that the water supply had failed. Bombs had broken water mains, and the reservoirs were emptying unchecked. Faced with this final disaster, Percival notified Wavell, who gave permission for the local commander to take whatever action he deemed necessary. Percival then called his staff together. They decided that surrender was the only alternative to total destruction of the city and the death of every person in it.

On February 15, Percival, with top members of his staff carrying a white flag, went to see Lieutenant General Tomoyuki Yamashita, commander of the Japanese invasion force. Back in Tokyo, Yamashita was hailed as "The Tiger of Malaya" for completing the conquest of the peninsula and Singapore a full month ahead of the timetable set by the Japanese Army's Imperial General Staff.

The first six months of Japanese occupation was a time of terror for Europeans and Chinese. As part of their campaign to discredit the white race in Asia, Japanese commanders undertook a campaign to humiliate their European prisoners. They also started a vendetta against the large number of Chinese in Singapore, a by-product of their war with China. The Japanese authorities suspected the local Chinese of spying for Chiang Kai-shek. A number of British prisoners were shipped to Thailand to work on the military railroad. This incident, years later, was the factual basis for the famous motion picture, *The Bridge on the River Kwai*.

One of the first Japanese actions under her "Asia for Asians" policy was to transfer Trengganu, Perlis, Kedah, and Kelantan back to the control of Thailand (Siam). The Thais established a Resident in these four Malay states but did not try to force any action on the sultans of any of the four Unfederated Malay States. In the four Federated States the Japanese professed to return full control to the sultans, but in actuality the native rulers had less freedom than under the British. The conquerors also tried to organize the Indians of Malaya into an "Indian National Army" to fight the British in Burma. Those who refused to join were conscripted into labor battalions.

The Malays received the best treatment under the Japanese occupation but suffered greatly from the resulting economic depression. The entrepôt trade declined alarmingly. Tin and rubber exports, vital to Malay economy, almost came to a standstill because much of the processing machinery was destroyed by the British during the retreat down the peninsula. Even after the mines were producing again, lack of shipping held up exports. The shipping crisis was caused by American submarine action which was aimed at depriving Japan of desperately needed rubber and tin.

The Japanese occupation was equally hard on the people of British Borneo. The enemy landed in the state of North Borneo (present Sabah) a week after the beginning of the attack on Malaya. They quickly overran North Borneo, Brunei, and Sarawak. Rajah Brooke, the third of the famous white rajahs, was in England at the time and did not return to Borneo until after the war. The conquerors left internal control in the hands of the sultans, but commandeered the oil from the rich fields in Brunei. In Sarawak the natives had grown used to the paternalistic rule of the Brooke rajahs and were bewildered by the turn of events. The Chinese in North Borneo, harshly treated by the Japanese, made contact with American guerrillas in the Philippines and helped organize a resistance group in Borneo. This organization led to an uprising against the Japanese in October 1943. North Borneo resistance fighters captured Jesselton, the state capital, and killed a number of Japanese. The resistance was put down with savage brutality. The Japanese used wholesale executions for the next six months to prevent new trouble.

After six months of uninterrupted victories, Japanese forces got their first setback in the Battle of the Coral Sea and then took another defeat in the Battle of Midway. These defeats were followed by American victories in New Guinea in 1943, when forces under General Douglas MacArthur began a slow move to retake the Philippine Islands. The war was turning against Japan. It now seemed to Japan a good idea to begin courting the favor of natives in the countries that Japan had occupied. To further this aim, in 1943 the Japanese established Malay advisory councils to assist the military governors. Since the Japanese generals refused to heed any advice, the plan was of little benefit.

Resistance to the Japanese occupation was organized under Communist direction. The Malayan Communist Party was organized in either 1927 or 1930—authorities differ. British law at the time required political bodies to register their constitutions and aims. The newly formed party had no intention of complying and operated as a secret organization during its early years. This is what makes it difficult to pinpoint both its organization date and its earlier operations. Communism did not appeal to the average Malay. The party drew most of its members from the Chinese and particularly the coolie class. Because of this, the British authorities did not consider the party much of a threat.

This attitude changed after Russia signed a non-aggression pact with Hitler's Germany in 1939. There were then 37,000 known Communists in the Federation of Malaya with about half of these in Singapore. They began a series of anti-British strikes that virtually stopped tin and rubber production. These strikes halted abruptly on direct orders from Moscow when Germany suddenly attacked Russia in June 1941. When Japan attacked Malaya in December 1941, the head of the Malayan Communist Party offered the party's full cooperation against the common enemy. Two hundred Communists who had had guerrilla training were supposed to stay behind the Japanese lines and disrupt communications as the enemy advanced. The plan failed. The Communists claimed the failure was caused by the

British not trusting them with demolition equipment. The British claimed that the Japanese advance was so swift that assistance could not be gotten to the guerrilla bands.

As soon as Singapore fell the Japanese started to eradicate the Communists. Party members fled into the jungles where they formed the Malayan People's Anti-Japanese Army, or MPAJA as it was popularly called. Most Malays were indifferent to MPAJA, but the Chinese population of Malaya almost to a man supported the guerrilla army with food, supplies, and intelligence about Japanese movements. The British Army in India parachuted in some supplies but were not too much interested in helping to build up a strong force because they knew that MPAJA was Communist controlled. By this time the war had progressed to the point where it appeared that the Allies would eventually win, and the British feared that the MPAJA would turn out to be a problem when the war ended. After considerable argument the MPAJA leaders agreed to register all weapons the British had smuggled in to them and to return them at the war's end. Even so, the MPAJA never became much of a threat to the Japanese occupation forces in Malaya.

The MPAJA forces continued to grow as more Chinese fled from the towns to escape Japanese persecution. By 1945 there were at least seven thousand members in the Malayan People's Anti-Japanese Army. After Japan's surrender in August 1945, following the atomic bombing of Hiroshima and Nagasaki, British administrative forces returned to Singapore in September. In keeping with their wartime agreement, MPAJA leaders disbanded the guerrilla army, and part of the weapons were returned. However, many of the guns parachuted in were reported lost or captured by the Japanese. In reality these were cached in the jungle awaiting the time when they could be used in a Communist-led revolt.

The Malayan Communist Party now came into the open, registering as a legal political group. Because Russia, England, and the United States had cooperated during the war, there was no valid reason under which the British authorities could ban the party even though it was no secret that the Malayan Communist Party was dedicated to ousting the British.

At this time there was little the Communists could do except develop future power in the Malayan labor unions operating in Singapore, Penang, Johore, and Malacca. There was no Malay support for the Party. Malayans in general had welcomed the return of the British. However, the war had destroyed Malayan faith in Great Britain. The entire British administration of Malaya from the beginning had been based upon "protection." The Malays now knew that British protection was not what they had thought it would be. As a result there was an increasing movement toward independence.

Nothing came from this growing nationalism immediately. The entire peninsula and the three Borneo states were in a miserable state. Malaria was rampant. Smallpox was again a danger, and other diseases reached epidemic proportions because of the complete breakdown of medical and sanitary facilities during the last days of the war. Crime reached the point where the cities were almost in a state of anarchy. The police force had declined under Japanese rule and was riddled with thieves and Japanese collaborators. Nothing could be done about this at first, for even a poor police force was better than none. Widespread unemployment that followed the end of the war added to the spread of crime. And in addition to the other troubles, there was a severe food shortage. Malaya's poor soil had not been able to produce sufficient food to feed her population since the expansion began in the fourteenth century. She had to depend on considerable imports, and food was in short supply all through Asia at this time.

Thailand (Siam) had collaborated with Japan by permitting Japanese troops free passage as the invaders moved toward Malaya at the beginning of the war. Great Britain now used this as an excuse to treat Thailand as a conquered nation, despite the heroic work done by the Thai underground for the Allies during the war. The United States tried to soften the harsh demands put on Thailand by Great Britain, but Prime Minister Churchill brushed American objections aside. He first demanded that Thailand provide several million tons of rice, cost free, for distribution in Malaya. This would have wrecked the Thai economy and probably caused a revolt of Thai rice farmers who would have received nothing for their crops. Finally after considerable pressure from the United States, Britain agreed to pay for the rice, but at a price below that of the world market. This eased the food shortage in Malaya.

Slow reconstruction added to Malaya's disillusionment with her British protectors. Before the war Malays showed little interest in politics. Rajahs fought with their sultans, primarily over succession, but the people showed little concern. They obeyed their leaders because they had always done so. Then the British loss of face and the growth of the Communist Party began to change this indifferent attitude. Political parties increased in number and size. In November 1945 Indonesians who envisioned absorbing Malaya into their nation as soon as the Dutch could be expelled backed a new Malay Nationalist Party. Then the Chinese formed the Malayan Democratic Union (MDU) to protect the interests of non-Malays. Friction between the Malays, Chinese, and Indian components of the Malayan population had increased during the war.

The British restored the Malayan government to its pre-war status. That is, the country was divided into three sections: the Federated States (Perak, Sengalor, Negri Sembilan, and Pahang); the Unfederated States (Perlis, Kedah, Trengganu, and Johore); and the Straits Settlements, which included Penang, Malacca, and Singapore. It quickly became apparent that British rule was in for a rough time. The Communist Party was pushing for a republic. The Nationalist Party wanted a union with Indonesia. The aims of the Chinese-dominated MDU were not stated, but increasing victories by Mao Tse-tung's Communist army in China indicated that soon heavy pressure would be put on Malaya's large Chinese population to support the victorious Red Chinese against Chiang Kai-shek. The size of the Chinese population of Malaya made this a distinct threat to the British in Southeast Asia.

Faced with this increasingly unstable situation, Great Britain proposed a Malay Union which would bring the three separate divisions of Malaya under a central control. Under this plan the chief executive officer would be a British-appointed governor and would be assisted by advisory councils. There would be one of these councils at each state level, with the state sultans presiding. These councils, however, could only advise. The actual handling of the government would be vested in executive and legislative councils. This plan would reduce the sultans, who had lost most of their power anyway, to the position of figureheads. Great Britain softened the blow as much as possible by announcing that the council system would be temporary. As soon as Malaya was ready, the British-dominated council government would be replaced with self-government. Angry Malay leaders believed this process would take about a hundred years. They were not willing to wait so long.

The first result of the Union proposal was to spur the formation of a new political party devoted to fighting the Malay Union. The new party was organized by Dato Onn bin Ja'afar of Johore who traveled about the country urging support for his United Malays National Organization (UMNO) and resistance to the Malay Union. Influential Englishmen in London also denounced the Union. Sir Frank Swettenham, who had long since retired to England, claimed that the Union imposed too much British control. The opposition reached the point where the British government abandoned the Union plan and instituted in its place the Federated plan which developed into the Federation of Malaya.

The Federation brought all Malay states except Singapore into one group, exactly as the Union proposed. The difference was primarily in greater recognition of states' rights. The sultans at last regained power and the British Resident was moved back to an advisory position again. The federal government was under a British High Commissioner, but his appointment had to be approved by the Malay sultans. Local government was entirely in the hands of the state governments, but the federal government could act to ensure uniform policies throughout the federation. A Conference of Rulers, consisting of the state sultans, was set up to meet three times a year. All amendments to the Federation constitution, immigration law changes, and appointment of senior government officials had to be ratified by this conference.

The Federation gave the Malays the greatest voice in their country's government since the establishment of the British protectorate system. However, there were restrictions on citizenship of non-Malays, and certain land reservations were made in favor of the Malay people which in effect made the Chinese and Indian minorities second-class citizens. Such actions laid the basis for the continuing strife that has wracked Malaya and its successor Malaysia to this very day.

CHAPTER NINE

Merdeka

THE years immediately following World War II saw the destruction of colonialism. India and Burma gained their independence from England. The Dutch lost Indonesia. And the French empire in Indochina was also lost to the demands for national independence. The demand for *merdeka*—freedom—came slower in Malaya than it did in the other countries of Southeast Asia, but it was no less sure. The British government realized this, and the Federation of Malaya was intended as a stop-gap measure to make the inevitable transition from colonialism to self-government as smooth as possible. British colonial policy was now to permit former colonies and protectorates to achieve independence within the framework of the British Commonwealth of Nations. Commonwealth nations, while politically independent, were pledged to mutual defense and trade agreements.

The Communists were not interested in the success of the Federation. They felt that it meant continued British domination of the peninsula. The Communist goal was a republic with Communist leadership. So two months after the Federation was formed in February 1948, the Communists began an intensive struggle against the new political arrangement. The men who had fought in the Malay Peoples' Anti-Japanese Army had been held together by an "Old Comrades" veterans' organization. Now former MPAJA leaders called back the veterans to serve the party again. Guerrilla warfare was resumed against the Federation and the British.

Guerrilla strategy involved first taking over a small area. Natives within the area were intimidated into giving full support. The initial small areas were gradually enlarged until they met other Communist-dominated areas. This gradual growth eventually permitted the takeover of entire states. Attacks were made on tin mines, rubber plantations, towns, and police stations. Most of the attacks were against Europeans, Indians, Chinese businessmen, and foreigners. The Malays were generally left alone, since the Communists were wooing their favor.

At first the federal government refused to believe that the increasing violence was Communist inspired. Officials blamed the disorder on criminal gangs formed during the breakdown of discipline in the final days of the Japanese occupation. But by June 1948 the evidence was overwhelming. An armed revolt was actually underway. The government hastily declared a state of national emergency on June 18, and six days later the government of the Crown Colony of Singapore followed suit.

British and Commonwealth troops from India and Australia were hastily shipped to Malaya. Mine and plantation owners organized their employees into shock troops to defend their property. Volunteer guard units were recruited to patrol and protect the *kampongs* (villages). Areas of Communist control were broken up, but the defending troops—although greatly outnumbering the Communists—could do little to stop the rebels' terrorist hit-and-run raids. The war dragged on for several years, with the Communists gradually losing ground.

In 1951 Onn bin Ja'afar, founder of the United Malays National Organization (UMNO) suddenly quit the political group to form a new one called the Independence of Malaya Party. Onn had become dissatisfied with the purely Malay nature of UMNO. He decided that no political group could succeed by representing just one of Malaya's ethnic groups. He wanted his new Malaya Independence Party to represent Malays, Chinese, and Indians. As it happened he drew support only from the Indians, and his political power declined.

As Onn was fading out of the political picture after making a brilliant start with his UMNO, his successor as head of the

United Malays National Organization, Tunku Abdul Rahman, became the new star in Malaya's political sky. Tunku means prince and Abdul Rahman was a member of the royalty of Kedah. As a young man he had studied law and was Assistant Government Prosecutor in the Federation government when he assumed the leadership of UMNO. The Tunku (in Malaysia he is almost universally called by his title instead of his name) lacked Onn's fire, but he was a much shrewder politician. He was friendly and tolerant, getting along well with all the races that make up modern Malaysia. Thus he made a good compromise leader whom all the parties could back. In 1953 the Tunku worked out an alliance with the Malayan Chinese Association and the Malayan Indian Congress that greatly strengthened his political hand.

The Alliance, as the coalition was known to the public, now announced independence as its national goal. By 1955 the Alliance was in control of the federal government with Tunku Abdul Rahman as prime minister. Once started, the independence movement moved swiftly. Great Britain still maintained control despite the great advances made in self-government, but she realized that independence for Malaya was inevitable.

The British finally agreed to permit complete independence for Malaya. "Merdeka" was proclaimed on August 31, 1957. The Duke of Gloucester came from England to personally represent Queen Elizabeth II at the ceremony. The duke presented the new nation's constitution to Tunku Abdul Rahman to symbolize the transfer of supreme authority from Great Britain to the new nation.

The constitution provided for a federation of Malay states headed by a prime minister. The nominal Head of State, who reigned but did not rule, was the *Yang di-Pertuan Agong* (Supreme Ruler). He was elected by the sultans of the nine original Malay states from their own ranks. The Supreme Ruler would serve for a five-year term and then would be replaced by another elected Yang di-Pertuan Agong. He would hold a ceremonial position comparable to that of the Queen of England. The prime minister and his cabinet would run the government according to laws passed by the Malayan parliament.

At the Merdeka ceremony the Duke of Gloucester read a

message to the Malayan people from her Majesty Queen Elizabeth: "I am confident that Malaya will respond worthily to the challenging tasks of independence and that she will continue to show to the world that example of moderation and goodwill toward all races that has been so marked a feature of her history."

Then Tunku Abdul Rahman, his voice shaking with emotion, read the Proclamation of Independence, saying: "I do hereby proclaim and declare that the Federation of Malaya is, and with God's blessing shall be forever, a sovereign democratic and independent State founded upon the principles of liberty and justice and ever seeking the welfare and happiness of its people and the maintenance of a just peace among all nations."

Then the Duke of Gloucester, the prime minister and the Yang di-Pertuan Agong saluted together as the flag of the new nation was raised.

The new independent nation was still at war with the Communist terrorist gangs in the jungles. Earlier the Communist leader Chan Peng had announced that the terrorists were only fighting for a free Malaya. Now that independence had been achieved, Tunku Abdul Rahman called on the guerrillas to stop fighting. Soon after the Merdeka ceremony Chan Peng asked for a meeting with the prime minister. The Tunku agreed, but refused the amnesty demands of the Communist leaders. The fighting dragged on for another two years, involving both Malay and British Commonwealth troops, for the independence agreement required the British government to give military assistance.

Gradually larger and larger groups of men deserted from the terrorist ranks. Chan Peng fled to sanctuary across the Thailand border. The fighting finally ceased in 1960. By this time the twelve-year jungle war had cost the lives of twelve thousand people, including both military and civilian. Shortly after the shooting stopped, Tunku Abdul Rahman lifted the state of emergency which had been proclaimed twelve years earlier.

Defeat in Malaya did not stop the Communist drive. Their main effort was merely transferred from the peninsula to Singapore, long the terrorists' chief supply base. Singapore had achieved the status of a self-governing state under British control and had its own miniature parliament. David Marshall, a native-born Singaporean of half-Jewish, half-Iraqi blood, became prime minister. He immediately began a drive for complete independence, but he was forced to resign the next year (1956) when his talks with the British ended in failure. He was succeeded by his friend Lim Yew-hock as prime minister. The main reason for Great Britain's refusal to grant Singapore full independence was the extreme danger of a Communist takeover if Britain relinquished control of security.

The new prime minister began a vigorous program to stamp out subversion. Communist organizations were suppressed. Demonstrations were brought under control. And a large number of Communists and their sympathizers were arrested. Great Britain was impressed by Lim's decisiveness and agreed to reopen talks about possible independence. The British government balked at going beyond the previous self-government concessions it had made to Singapore, claiming that the 224-square-mile island was too weak to defend itself alone. The opinion was expressed to Lim during one of his trips to London that independence would be granted only if Singapore could ally itself with Malaya. The Tunku refused to consider joining Singapore with Malaya.

As the arguments for full independence for Singapore continued, preparations were made for the first fully free elections under the self-governing constitution. It quickly became apparent that Lim Yew-hock and his government were in serious trouble with the voters. The rising star in Singapore politics was a young Chinese lawyer named Lee Kuan Yew. Lee had been a founder of the People's Action Party (PAP) which was accused of being a Communist-front organization. Despite the fact that several of its top members were in jail, PAP easily won the election, taking 43 out of 51 seats in the Assembly.

Lee, as leader of the winning party, was invited by Sir William Goode, Governor-General of Singapore, to form a government under the parliamentary system. While Goode may have had misgivings about Lee Kuan Yew, under the constitution granting self-government the governor had no choice. Lee, however, refused to form a government unless PAP members in jail were released. Governor Goode agreed and Lee became prime minister, heading the government of Singapore. Goode, as provided in the agreement for self-government, resigned as governor and was transferred to Borneo. Singapore, despite its self-governing status, was still a part of the British Empire, and agitation continued for full independence.

Lee Kuan Yew surprised both friend and foe. He acknowledged that there were Communists in his party, but disavowed communism himself. He professed to be a Socialist, which also frightened Singapore's merchants. Socialism is government regulation of business as well as other essentials of a nation's well-being. Singapore had no industry of any importance. It existed solely on its earnings as a free port of trade. Socialist regulation would stifle a port like Singapore. Because merchants, unlike big industries, do not have enormous plants which are difficult to move, they can shift their bases of operations with ease. The Dutch found this out when they tried to regulate trade in Malacca after taking the city from the Portuguese, at which time Malaccan merchants moved to Singapore. However, Lee Kuan Yew—while professing Socialistic leanings and admitting Communist support—very effectively stifled Communist attempts to take over the island and has maintained Singapore's free port status.

When elections came up again in 1961, Lee frankly admitted to the people of Singapore that he had accepted Communist support, but added, "The PAP is one of the few groups that have worked in a united front with the Malayan Communist Party and have not been absorbed into it." And it was true. As Harry Miller, former chief reporter (the newspaper's designation) for the *Straits Times*, put it: "Lee gained the confidence of business—local and overseas—by demonstrating competence, integrity of purpose and freedom from corruption." These qualities not only solidified Lee's position, but have kept him in office despite some serious crises that have rocked his island city-state.

From the beginning Lee urged unification of Singapore with Malaya. The British also favored the union, repeating their stand that full independence for Singapore would not come until such unification was achieved. Lee pointed out that 41 percent of Malaya's imports moved through Singapore and that 31 percent of her exports were also handled by Singapore's ports. Tunku Abdul Rahman, while professing friendship for Singapore, still refused to permit unification of the two countries. The Tunku denied being afraid that Singapore's one and a half million

Chinese would outbalance the Malays if Singapore was permitted to join the Federation of Malaya.

The Tunku explained his position in a later speech in which he said, "I was of the opinion that integration of the two territories would spell trouble—trouble for all of us, trouble for this country and the security part of our lives. The differences in outlook of the people of the Federation and Singapore were so pronounced that for me a merger at that time was out of the question."

He mentioned religion—Islam in Malaya and predominantly Buddhism in Singapore—and the Malay language in contrast to the Chinese language as examples of these differences.

"In the event of a merger of the two territories, the different views of the people of the Federation and Singapore might clash, and clash violently."

Then, beginning in 1961, the political situation in Singapore took a turn that disturbed the Tunku, and he began to view the situation in Singapore as a future threat to Malaya. In another speech to his people Tunku Abdul Rahman reviewed the background that led to his change of position toward union between Malaya and Singapore:

"After the election of 1959 Singapore tried to set up an extreme Socialist Government under the party called PAP . . . Businessmen of Singapore had their own misgivings and fears about the extreme Socialist policy—they were transferring their interests into the Federation of Malaya. This was serious for Singapore, bearing in mind that the economy of the island rests solely on business, trade, and commerce." He went on to say that Lee Kuan Yew found it difficult to run the island's government without the cooperation of businessmen and that Singapore was in danger of destroying itself by driving away the commerce upon which its economy was built. "The responsible leaders then realized that they owed a duty to the people rather than to themselves. So the seeds of difference between the non-Communist elements and the pro-Communist elements in PAP were sown."

PAP was a coalition of several political elements. When Prime Minister Lee Kuan Yew broke with his Communist supporters, he lost considerable support. Though his party won in the 1961 elections, retaining control of the government, the Tunku was frightened by the election in Malaya, for it indicated that there was a distinct possibility that Singapore would go Communist in the future. A Communist Singapore could well be a disaster for Malaya in the next confrontation between Malaya and the Malayan Communist Party.

"The division of Singapore and Malaya might be all right while Singapore is under control of Great Britain. But a time will come when Singapore will be given independence—I have no doubt they will be given independence—and that time is not far off and new talks will be held in 1963," the Tunku told the Malayan parliament.

With this situation facing him, the Tunku was now ready to admit Singapore into the Federation of Malaya, provided he could assure himself that the island's large Chinese population—one and a half million—would not upset the racial balance in Malaya and permit the Chinese to dominate Federation politics. He knew very well how ambitious and brilliant Lee Kuan Yew was. The Tunku could envision Lee one day becoming prime minister of the Federation of Malaya.

Still the Tunku was convinced that Malaya's future security depended upon taking Singapore into the union. After considerable secret discussions with his own ministers and with Lee Kuan Yew, the Tunku finally approved a plan he thought would solve the problems of union with Singapore. Instead of taking Singapore into the Federation, the Federation would be dissolved and replaced with a completely new nation to be called Malaysia.

To counterbalance the large number of Malaysians of Chinese origin who would come into the new union with the admission of Singapore, the Tunku called for the admission also of the Malay states under domination of the British in Borneo. These were North Borneo State (now Sabah), Brunei, and Sarawak. This, Tunku Abdul Rahman thought, would ensure Malay predominance in the new nation.

It appeared to be a masterly solution to a difficult problem. However, the Tunku failed to take into consideration three factors that proved later to be vital. One was the opposition of the ancient sultanate of Brunei to joining the new nation. Another was the driving ambition of Lee Kuan Yew. And the third factor which would cause serious trouble was the surprising objection of the Philippine Islands and of the new nation of Indonesia.

Malaysia was in trouble before it was even formed.

CHAPTER TEN

Trials of a New Nation

ONCE the Tunku made his decision to bring about the merger of Malaya, the British Borneo states, and Singapore into the new nation of Malaysia, he moved swiftly to get domestic and international support for his plan. This began with a "trial balloon" issued as a feeler to test response. The feeler was dropped in a casual manner as part of a speech the Malayan prime minister made to the Foreign Correspondents' Association of Southeast Asia at a meeting in Singapore on May 27, 1961.

In the course of the speech the Tunku said, "Malaya today as a nation realizes that she cannot stand alone and in isolation . . . Sooner or later she should have an understanding with Britain and the peoples of Singapore, Borneo, Brunei, and Sarawak. It is premature for me to say how this closer understanding can be brought about, but it is inevitable that we should look ahead to this objective and think of a plan whereby these territories can be brought closer together in a political and economic cooperation."

Reaction to this feeler was good in Malaya and Singapore. There was less acceptance in Borneo. The three states there felt that they would be only exchanging British overlordship for Malayan domination. The states of North Borneo and Sarawak had earlier suggested a federation of the Borneo states, but Brunei resisted both a Borneo federation and the proposed nation of Malaysia. The Sultan of Brunei had but recently achieved self-government, and his country was doing well because of royalties from rich oil deposits.

Great Britain, however, pushed hard for the union with Malaya and Singapore. Her position was much like that of the old East India Company in its first dealings with the Malay Peninsula. Direct administration of colonies was too expensive, and growing nationalism promised nothing but trouble for imperialistic nations in the future. Britain hoped that by freeing all her colonies and retaining them as independent members of the British Commonwealth, she could still have her trade advantages without the expense of administration. However, the Communist push in the Far East, plus the greed of Indonesia and the Philippine Islands, revealed that any small country with desires for independence would soon fall under the domination of a stronger neighbor or be taken over by the Communists. Federation of Malaya and Singapore would solve this problem, creating a stronger nation which would be able—with Commonwealth defense treaties—to protect its independence.

The first public reaction of Borneo officials was a total rejection of the merger plan. This reaction began to change after a regional conference of delegates from Malaya and Borneo met in Singapore on July 21, 1961, less than two months after the Tunku's speech to the correspondents launched the idea of a merger. A high level committee met early in 1962 to determine if such a merger would be to the advantage of Borneo states. The group was called the Cobbold Commission after its chairman, Lord Cobbold, a former governor of the Bank of England.

The Cobbold Commission reported that the merger was in the interest of the Borneo states because of the difficult world situation. At the same time the Commission tried to find a compromise for the ticklish questions of state sovereignty and religion. Under the Malayan constitution only a sultan of one of the original nine Malay states could be elected Supreme Ruler (Yang di-Pertuan Agong). The two states formed from part of the original British Straits Settlements were barred from this honorary position. The Commission recommended that the bar be held for Sarawak and North Borneo, but that the Sultan of Brunei be made eligible for election to the high post.

On other disputed questions the Commission said, "It is

agreed that the three Borneo territories should have certain local safeguards in respect to colonization, taxation, customs and fiscal matters." On the subject of religion, the Commission said, "A great deal of attention was directed to the question of Islam, as the religion of the Federation. It is satisfied that the acceptance of Islam as the religion of the Federation will not endanger religious freedom within Malaysia." The report went on to point out that the present constitution of Malaya contained definite safeguards respecting freedom of religion and other personal freedoms.

Work on resolving problems continued throughout 1962. By the end of the year it appeared that the formation of Malaysia was nearing reality. However, in December 1962 a revolt broke out in Brunei, led by Sheikh A. M. Azahari, who founded the Rakyat Party. Azahari had long been an ardent anti-colonialist and a bitter foe of the British. At the end of World War II Azahari fought with the Indonesians in their war for independence from the Dutch. He returned to Brunei in 1952 and soon after formed the Rakyat political party. Azahari had remained sympathetic to his Indonesian friends, and Indonesia, through its firebrand president Sukarno, had expressed great displeasure at the plan to take the British Borneo states into the proposed nation of Malaysia. Azahari wanted to mold North Borneo, Brunei, and Sarawak into a new nation called North Kalimantan under Indonesian influence. Indonesia now controlled all of Borneo except the British states and had renamed the island Kalimantan.

When it appeared that Malaysia would be formed, Azahari began a revolt in Brunei and adjacent areas of Sarawak and North Borneo. He did not lead the action himself, but went to the Philippines. After the rebels seized several strong points, including the Shell Oil Company's fields, Azahari announced from Manila that he was the new "prime minister of the Revolutionary State of North Kalimantan." Unfortunately for Azahari's plans to force a union of the Borneo states, a company of Indian troops, followed by military forces from the other Commonwealth nations, smashed the revolt in ten days.

The Sultan of Brunei declared martial law and suspended the assembly because of the large number of Azahari supporters in its membership. In Malaya the Tunku assailed Indonesia for supporting the rebels. President Sukarno of Indonesia denounced the Tunku and denied that Indonesia officially supported the Brunei rebels, although he admitted that "all Indonesia sympathizes with the people of northern Kalimantan [Borneo] in their struggle for freedom." Sukarno then began a systematic denunciation of the proposed Malaysia treaty, calling it a plot to encircle Indonesia and to save Borneo's natural resources for the benefit of imperialistic nations.

Even more surprising to Malaysia than Indonesia's attitude was an attack by the Philippine Islands on the principles of the Malaysia treaty. President Macapagal of the Philippines objected to the inclusion of North Borneo in the new nation, because, he claimed, the territory had been illegally ceded to Baron Von Overbeck and Alfred Dent, founders of the North Borneo Company, which later ceded the territory to Great Britain. The founders of the North Borneo Company, afraid of future claims, had made two treaties. One was with the local sultan in North Borneo, and the other was with the Sultan of Sulu because of the sultan's claims on the territory.

President Macapagal claimed that even if the Sultan of Sulu had a right to sign the treaty, it was not his intention to make a permanent gift of the land but only to give the company limited trading privileges. The *London Times* refuted this claim by quoting from the original treaty-deed: "On behalf of ourselves, our heirs and successors we hereby grant and cede of our own free will and sovereign will to Gustavus, Baron Von Overbeck and Alfred Dent, Esq., as representatives of a British Company forever and in perpetuity all rights and powers belonging to us on the mainland of Borneo."

Faced with this definite statement of intent, the Philippine president then insisted that the Sultan of Sulu had had no right to cede the territory. When the treaty had been made with the North Borneo Company, the Philippine Islands were under Spanish jurisdiction, and Spain, not the Sultan of Sulu, had sovereignty over North Borneo. This claim was refuted by a treaty signed in 1885 between Spain and Britain in which Spain recognized British right in Borneo and Britain renounced any claim to the Sulu islands.

As further evidence against the Philippine claim to North Borneo, the British Foreign Office pointed out that the United States had replaced Spain in the Philippines after the Spanish-American War of 1898. The United States had then formally recognized British claims to North Borneo in a convention signed in 1930. The Philippine counterclaim insisted that an independent nation such as the Philippine Islands could not be bound by agreements made by the colonial governments that preceded it.

In the meantime, Sukarno of Indonesia continued to fight the union of Malay states as a distinct threat to his own plans for expansion. At one point he said that Indonesia would withdraw her objection to the North Borneo states joining Malaysia if a United Nations Commission would conduct an investigation to certify that the people of the three states, North Borneo, Sarawak, and Brunei, did wish to join in the proposed Malaysia federation. At first Great Britain objected to the United Nations intervening in the Malaysian dispute, but finally she agreed.

At the same time that Sukarno was saying that he would withdraw objections if the United Nations certified the federation, he and President Macapagal of the Philippines endorsed a loose federation of all the Southeast Asian countries with predominantly Malayan people. This federation, in which each member nation would retain its independence, was to be called Maphilindo—a curious name created by taking the first letters of Malaya, the Philippines, and Indonesia. The plan never received serious consideration.

Meanwhile, Sarawak and North Borneo agreed to join the Malaysian federation, but in June 1963 Brunei announced that she would never join. The negotiator had agreed to permit the Sultan of Brunei to become part of the royal circle from which the supreme ruler would be elected, but the negotiations broke down over the question of oil royalties from public land in Brunei. The Tunku agreed to permit Brunei to continue collecting the royalties for the next ten years, but after that time the money would go into the Malaysian treasury. This was totally unacceptable to Brunei, and the Sultan announced that his tiny country would remain a self-governing member of the British Commonwealth.

At a meeting in London, Great Britain, Malaya, and Singapore agreed that the new nation of Malaysia would be created and become effective on August 31, 1963. This date had to be postponed to permit the United Nations Commission to make its study and report to U Thant, the United Nations Secretary-General. Then both Indonesia and the Philippines insisted that they be permitted to send observers with the United Nations group. Great Britain agreed, but President Sukarno stalled again. This time he insisted that Indonesia be allowed to increase its ten observers to thirty. The demand was refused and both the Philippines and Indonesia withheld their observers for ten days before giving in and sending them to join the inquiry. This incident gave Sukarno another excuse to blast the United Nations, Great Britain, and the plan to form Malaysia.

The Commission announced that it would render its report on September 14, 1963. The Malayan government, in concurrence with the Borneo States, Singapore, and Great Britain, then announced that the nation of Malaysia would be formed on September 16. This action angered United Nations Secretary-General U Thant, for the Commission had not yet concluded its investigation and the Secretary-General viewed the announcement as a declaration that Malaya and Great Britain were contemptuous of the United Nations and did not care what the investigation revealed.

Meanwhile, Indonesia stepped up military action along the 1,000-mile front between Kalimantan (Indonesian Borneo) and the British Borneo states. Guerrilla bands penetrated into the states of North Borneo, Sarawak, and Brunei. Sukarno did not admit that these were regular Indonesian forces, but tried to preserve the fiction that they were remnants of the rebels who had supported Azahari's attempt to overthrow the Sultan of Brunei.

August 31, 1963, had been the intended date for the creation of Malaysia before the postponement for the United Nations survey. The governments of Sarawak, North Borneo, and Singapore had objected to the postponement. These governments now decided to keep the original date for their declarations of independence as a means of dramatizing their objection to the delay and to what they felt was unwarranted United Nations interference in their activities. So on August 31 Lee Kuan Yew issued a proclamation declaring Singapore's independence from Great Britain and stating that his island city-state would conduct its own foreign policy and defense until Malaysia was created. Up to this time Great Britain had conducted Singapore's foreign relations and defense from the great Singapore naval base, although Singapore was self-governing in all other respects.

Sarawak and North Borneo also chose the 31st of August as the time to put into effect the governments that they would have under the Malaysian federation. North Borneo then changed her name to Sabah. These actions increased Sukarno's rage. While arguments continued, a new enemy of Malaysia suddenly appeared. The Pan-Malayan Islamic Party of Kelantan, the Malayan state on the east coast of the peninsula, asked the Supreme Court of Malaya to stop the Tunku from taking the Federation of Malaya into the new nation of Malaysia. The party, which controlled the government of Kelantan state, was strongly pro-Malay. It feared the introduction of the large Chinese population of Singapore into a union with Malaya. The court rejected the petition on the grounds that the states of the Federation of Malaya had no authority to object to the actions of the federal government and that there was no need for the federal government to consult the states when acting for the common welfare.

As the date neared for the delivery of the United Nations report, Indonesia stepped up her anti-British campaign. Events made it obvious that Sukarno had no intention of abiding by his statement—made at Manila in July—that he would accept a United Nations Commission finding concerning the desires of the people of Borneo about joining the union of Malaysia. On September 12 an Indonesian mob tore down the British flag at the British Consulate in Surabaya in northeastern Java. Then the UN Commission report was issued on September 14, and— as expected—was favorable to the creation of the new nation of Malaysia.

In concluding his report of the Commission's findings to the General Assembly of the United Nations, U Thant said: "From the beginning of this year [1963], I have been observing the rising tension in Southeast Asia on account of the difference of opinion among the countries most directly interested in the Malaysia issue. It was in hope that some form of United Nations involvement might help to reduce tension that I agreed to respond positively to the request made by the three Manila powers [i.e., Malaya, the Philippines, and Indonesia]. I would hope that the exercise in which my colleagues and I [the UN inquiry mission to Borneo] have been involved in this regard would have this effect, and that the coming into being of Malaysia will not prove to be a continuing source of friction and tension in this area."

U Thant was not to get his wish for a lessening of tension. Instead the situation exploded in greater violence. The formation of Malaysia was formally proclaimed on September 16, 1963. The next day representatives of the fourteen states making up the new nation met at Merdeka Stadium in Kuala Lumpur, the national capital. This was the same location where, six years earlier, Tunku Abdul Rahman had proclaimed the independence of Malaya. Indonesia and Philippine representatives were not among the diplomats from foreign nations who assembled for the ceremonies. They were recalled by their governments. The Tunku retaliated by ordering Malaysian ambassadors to leave the Philippines and Indonesia, breaking diplomatic relations.

In concluding his address to the assembly, Tunku Abdul Rahman said: "Malaysia shall by the grace of God, the Lord of the Universe, forever be an independent and sovereign State founded upon liberty and justice, ever seeking to defend and uphold peace and harmony among its people and to perpetuate peace among nations."

The Tunku's hope for peace and harmony among Malaysia's people proved as vain as U Thant's hope that tension would lessen in Southeast Asia after the UN Commission rendered its report. Indonesia observed Malaysia Declaration Day with uprisings against British citizens in Djakarta and by more savage guerrilla attacks in Borneo. Sukarno called the new attacks "Confrontation," and announced that his aim was to "crush Malaysia." He kept repeating that Malaysia was a threat to Indonesia. In actuality the only threat was to Sukarno's personal ambition to control all the Malay world himself.

While Malaysia was in truth a new nation, officially it was not acknowledged as such. The Tunku called it an expansion of the old Federation of Malaya even though a new name and constitution were introduced. This was done for practical political reasons. By calling Malaysia an expansion of Malaya, the Tunku did not have to seek new diplomatic recognition from foreign nations or new membership in the United Nations nor did he have to replace missions.

Various Asian and European nations tried to mediate the Malaysia-Indonesia dispute, but none were successful. In January 1963 President John F. Kennedy of the United States sent his brother Robert to Indonesia to talk with Sukarno. Kennedy was no more successful than previous diplomats. In fact, the trouble intensified after Kennedy's visit. It was as if Sukarno suspected possible American intervention and intended to crush Malaysia before this happened. Such a fear was ill founded, for the United States was becoming more involved in Vietnam and was in no position to extend her involvement into Malaysia, Borneo, and Indonesia.

The British came immediately to Malaysia's aid in accordance with a defense treaty which was part of the independence agreement. British and Commonwealth troops were moved into Borneo, for up to this point the actual shooting phase of the "Confrontation" had been restricted to the frontier between Malaysia's Borneo states and Indonesia's Kalimantan. Then in August 1964 Sukarno landed a force of one hundred men on the southwest shore of Johore state at the tip of the Malay Peninsula. The landing party was supposed to furnish a nucleus for a jungle guerrilla band which would draw new members from Indonesian sympathizers in Malaysia.

The infiltration plan failed and Malaysian police and soldiers quickly rounded up the landing force. Sukarno was not daunted. He followed up this invasion of West Malaysia with another hundred Indonesian guerrillas who were parachuted into Johore. Again Sukarno had overestimated the number of Indonesian sympathizers in the Malay state. The guerrillas were turned in by loyal Malays and arrested before they could set up operations.

Sukarno at first angrily denied that the two invasions were inspired by Indonesia. He insisted that they were independent

Trials of a New Nation

"freedom fighters." Malaysia retaliated by making a complaint to the United Nations Security Council. In the debate that followed, the Indonesian delegate to the UN reiterated Indonesia's claim that the formation of Malaysia was a British plot to enslave all Malay people and thereby was a direct threat to Indonesia's future.

The Malaysian delegate charged that the paratroopers dropped into Johore were regular members of the Indonesian forces and that the plane used was a Hercules (American-built) transport from the Indonesian Air Force. In addition the paratroopers included ten Malaysian Chinese Communists who had been selected to serve as guides for the infiltrating guerrillas. Two of the Chinese were women. The Malaysian delegate displayed a large amount of ammunition and equipment seized after the landing. Many of the grenades, detonators, and packages of TNT bore Indonesian markings. The Russian delegate was chairing the Security Council meeting on this occasion, and he demanded that the munitions be removed because of danger to the other delegates.

The Indonesian delegate continued to denounce the British, saying: "Since Indonesia's independence, my country and my people have suffered much from colonialism and imperialism. The neighboring areas, which are now called Malaysia, inhabited by our brother peoples, have been used by British colonialism as a base from which to challenge, to fight, and to subvert our Republic, our Revolution, politically, economically, and militarily."

The delegate went on to say that Indonesia had never been against the formation of Malaysia, but what she objected to was the formation of a Malaysia dominated by the British. The Indonesian actually meant that the objection was to the British defense agreement. The presence of British forces in Malaysia would prevent Sukarno's expansion plans. The Indonesian dictator hoped first to absorb the former British Borneo states into Kalimantan (Indonesian Borneo) and then to dominate or take over the peninsular Malay states at a later date.

The Indonesian delegate, Suwardjo Tjondonegro, went on to insist that the defense arrangements between Malaysia and Britain were a subterfuge to permit Great Britain to meddle in the affairs of all Southeast Asia under the guise of "preserving peace." He added that Indonesia would not have objected to the formation of Malaysia "if it had been founded on the cooperative will for freedom of the peoples in Southeast Asia rather than on the power and protection of Britain."

He ended by admitting for the first time that some of the guerrillas fighting in northern Borneo had been trained in Indonesia, but insisted that British and Malaysian troops in Borneo had also violated Indonesian territory.

The evidence left no question that Indonesia was definitely the aggressor. However, the Security Council failed to take a positive stand for fear of a Russian veto of any condemnation of Indonesia. This veto was assured for two reasons. One, it would be a slap at world democracy. Secondly, the People's Republic of China through its Communist groups in Southeast Asia was developing considerable influence in this area, and Russia wanted to woo Indonesian goodwill to offset the Chinese, who were becoming increasingly at odds with Russia.

Finally a watered-down resolution introduced by Norway was passed, with Russia and Czechoslovakia voting against it. The resolution merely "took note of the Malaysia complaint" regarding the Indonesian landings on the Malay Peninsula, expressed "deep concern by armed incidents in that region which have seriously aggravated the situation," and "deplored the incidents which form the basis of the complaint."

Then the resolution requested the parties concerned to make every effort to avoid a recurrence of such incidents; called upon them to refrain from "all threat and use of force and to respect the territorial and political independence of each other"; and finally recommended that Indonesia and Malaysia resume their talks on a diplomatic level.

The resolution might be considered a moral victory for Malaysia, but from a practical standpoint it was worthless. This resolution underscored the futility of United Nations actions to settle international difficulties of small nations when the giant world powers take opposing sides.

CHAPTER ELEVEN

A Nation in Danger

CONFRONTATION continued. Indonesian guerrilla forces continued to attack the Malay Peninsula. At the same time Indonesian-trained Malaysians of both Malay and Chinese extraction started riots in Malaysia cities. One of the most serious occurred in July 1964 as the Muslims were celebrating the birthday of the Prophet Mohammed. Thiry-five people were killed and more than a thousand rioters were arrested in Singapore.

The opening of 1965 brought a new turn in the hostilities. It was Malaysia's turn to take a temporary seat on the United Nation's Security Council, alternating a two-year term with Czechoslovakia. Sukarno threatened to withdraw Indonesia from the world body if Malaysia were permitted to take the Security Council seat. The threat was ignored by the UN, and Indonesia resigned. (She was reinstated the next year, 1966).

It became apparent that Sukarno was motivated by something other than anger at the seating of Malaysia. Malaysia could have taken no action on the Security Council that would have endangered Indonesia, for Russia would have vetoed any such move. Sukarno simply used the seating as an excuse to withdraw. He was planning a new and stronger attack on the Malaysian states in Borneo and did not want to be hampered by United Nations membership. The Tunku was alarmed by the turn of

103

events and appealed to the Security Council for assistance should Indonesia attack in force. Until this time the fighting had been among small guerrilla groups. The UN reaction was not too favorable. To make matters worse for the Tunku, who was an avowed anti-Communist, the Indonesian Communist Party appeared to be on the verge of gaining enough strength to take over Indonesia.

Then more trouble developed closer to home. The Tunku suddenly became fearful of the ambitious Lee Kuan Yew in Singapore. It will be recalled that the Tunku had been afraid to admit Singapore to the original Federation of Malaya because of the effect such a large number of Chinese (nearly one and a half million) would have on the nation's elections. He thought the inclusion of North Borneo Malays would offset this and finally agreed to include Singapore in the Malaysian federation. Now it appeared that he had made a mistake.

The Tunku's government held power through the "Alliance Party," a coalition of the United Malays National Organization UMNO (the Tunku's party), the Malayan Chinese Association, and the Malayan Indian Congress. The Malayan Chinese Association (MCA) had always distrusted Lee Kuan Yew and his People's Action Party (PAP). Lee was known as an ardent Socialist, and his PAP party was acknowledged to have Communist members. The Malayan Chinese Association, on the other hand, was composed of middle-class Chinese living on the peninsula away from Singapore where Lee had his influence. These peninsular Chinese were primarily interested in getting along with their Malay neighbors and wanted nothing to disturb their businesses.

In the 1964 elections, the first held since the formation of Malaysia, Lee Kuan Yew set out to directly challenge the MCA. His objective was to get members of his own PAP party elected to seats held by MCA members and thus increase the pressure he and his PAP top officials could put on the Tunku. Lee won only one seat in the Assembly by this maneuver but gained the enmity of powerful Malay politicians.

Lee's action in the election caused the Tunku to take a hard second look at this enterprising Chinese politician. The Chinese population of Malaysia, including Singapore and the Borneo

States, was about 47 percent of the total. If Lee could swing the total Chinese vote and the Indian vote as well, the Chinese-Indian coalition could sweep the Malays out of power in their own country. Even though these Chinese had been in Malaysia for generations, the Malays had never looked upon them as natives. They remained Chinese and the Indians remained Indians, both nationalities separated from the Malays by race, customs, ideals, and religion. Even if a Chinese citizen's father and grandfather had been born in Malaya, he still remained a foreigner and an interloper in the eyes of the Malays.

Such an attitude was an open invitation to dissension. Stern British discipline had prevented trouble in the past, but the British were gone now and the Malays controlled the government. The Chinese had begun to settle in Malaya only after the British established trading centers in Penang and Singapore. Then expansion of the tin mining industry had brought a great migration of Chinese. Chinese industry and ability to amass wealth irritated the Malays, who were by nature a more easygoing people, lacking the intense drive for success that motivated the Chinese. Then the bloody riots of the mid-1880s when Chinese secret societies fought each other had further alienated the Malays.

Malayan fear and distrust of the Chinese were clearly reflected in the constitution drawn up when Malaya got her independence from Britain. This discrimination was then carried over into the Malaysian constitution. Restrictions on citizenship were included that favored the Malay population over the other two nationalities. Chinese language classes could no longer be conducted in Chinese secondary schools. The language of instruction had to be either Malay or English. In addition certain "Malay rights" were written into the constitution. These are rather complex but can be summarized as placing restrictions on the number of Chinese and Indians who can be employed in the Malaysian civil service or who can serve in the Malaysian armed forces. Government scholarship awards for students are under the same national quota system. And large areas of public land are set aside as "Malay reservations." Only Malays are permitted to own land within choice reservation areas.

While not spelled out in the constitution, as are the other

restrictions, there also seems to be an unofficial—but none the less strict—quota system for establishing new businesses and obtaining franchises. John Slimming, a British reporter, notes that a Chinese taxi operator in Kuala Lumpur told him that one-third of the taxi company's profit had to be turned over to a Malay front man for the use of the Malay's name as the official owner of the company.

These restrictions do not outwardly bother established Chinese businessmen in Malaysia. Although as a result they are barred from taking a prominent place in the government, they do not care who rules as long as they can pursue their businesses. As a result, the Malayan Chinese Association party was glad to join the Alliance coalition with the Tunku's United Malays National Organization party. Middle-class Chinese only wanted to preserve what they had.

Lee Kuan Yew had an opposing view. He did not draw his political strength from what he called "the Capitalist Chinese," but from the dock workers and poorer classes in Singapore who were attracted by his socialist leanings. Lee angrily denounced the MCA Chinese for their willingness to be second-class citizens and asserted that he supported equality for all races in Malaysia. After the election went against him, Lee made a new move aimed directly at breaking the Malay grip on the federal government. He organized a "Malaysia Solidarity Convention" with the intention of bringing together all Malaysian people outside the Malays. If this could be done, then Lee would have a majority of voters on his side.

The Convention flatly called for a "Malaysian Malaysia." What this meant was spelled out in an inaugural speech by Lee in which he said, "A Malaysian Malaysia means that the nation and the State are not identified with the supremacy, well-being and interests of any one community or race. A Malaysian Malaysia is the antithesis of a Malay Malaysia, a Chinese Malaysia, a Dayak Malaysia, an Indian Malaysia and so on. The special and legitimate rights of different communities must be secured and promoted within the framework of the collective rights, interests and responsibilities of all races."

The inaugural address went on to say that those who supported the concept of a Malaysian Malaysia were "determined to unite and work for its realization no matter how arduous and protracted the struggle may be."

The Malay population naturally reacted strongly to Lee's declaration. The long-standing enmity between the Chinese and the Malays was fanned into a greater flame. There was an uproar in parliament where angry speeches denounced Lee for trying to take away "Malay rights." The Tunku had gone to England to attend a Commonwealth Prime Ministers' Conference in early May, prior to Lee's call for a Malaysian Malaysia. In fact, there is some suspicion that Lee Kuan Yew deliberately timed his Malaysian Solidarity Convention to coincide with the Tunku's absence from the country.

The Tunku was naturally informed of Lee's attack on "Malay rights" but fell ill and had to go to the south of France to recuperate. He did not return to Malaysia until early August. In the meantime a war of words went on, with angry leaders on both sides denouncing the other race. The Malays were warned about Chinese control of the economy and told how Chinese members of the wartime Malayan People's Anti-Japanese Army had killed many Malays for alleged collaboration with the Japanese. The Chinese in turn were warned by their leaders that the Malays intended to destroy them.

There were demands in the Malaysian parliament that troops be sent to Singapore to arrest Lee as a traitor. In Europe Tunku Abdul Rahman realized that the situation had been blown up by both sides to the point where the breach was too wide ever to be repaired. With this certainty in mind, the Tunku returned to Kuala Lumpur in the first week of August 1965 with his plan of action. On his arrival at the Malaysian capital, the Tunku was asked by newspapermen if he intended to confer with Lee Kuan Yew. The Tunku replied soothingly that as soon as he settled down he would certainly do so.

While the Tunku's statement was moderate and seemingly without rancor, as were all his public statements, the Malaysian deputy prime minister, Tun Razak, stated flatly: "I must warn Mr. Lee that although we stand for racial harmony, for goodwill and peace and unity, if as a result of his adventure, trouble should break out in this country, we must hold him responsible."

He went on to denounce Lee for "blackening the image of

our country in the eyes of our friends abroad, creating doubt and suspicions among the minds of our peoples, and undermining the goodwill and harmony of the various races" while "we are faced with a threat to our independence and sovereignty from outside." The outside threat referred to was the continuing Indonesian Confrontation.

Tunku Abdul Rahman returned to Kuala Lumpur on August 5, and on August 6 he and Lee had their fateful meeting. Lee, along with the general public, assumed that the Tunku would try to find a middle ground upon which the Malays and Chinese could agree. Instead, the Malaysian prime minister laid down an ultimatum. The stunned Lee was told he had two alternatives. One was an armed intervention into Singapore, removing Lee and his sympathizers. The second was the withdrawal of Singapore from the Malaysian Federation. There was nothing Lee could do to change the Tunku's decision—which apparently had been made before the prime minister left Europe. An agreement to the secession of Singapore from Malaysia was drawn up and signed on the evening of Saturday, August 7, 1965.

The agreement to expel Singapore was made in such secrecy that the British were totally unaware of it until the public announcement was made on Monday, August 9. Lee read the announcement at ten o'clock in Singapore, while Tunku Abdul Rahman made the announcement to the Malaysian parliament at the same time in Kuala Lumpur.

In his address the Tunku said that the only alternative to the secession of Singapore was "to take repressive measures against the Singapore government for the behavior of some of their leaders." He then added: "We feel that repressive measures against a few would not solve the problem because the seed of this contempt, fear and hatred has been sown in Singapore. Even if we try to prevent its growth, I feel that after a time it will sprout up with more virulent force."

The separation was hailed with joy in Kuala Lumpur but with dismay in Singapore. Singapore, because of its small size, would be almost defenseless against foreign aggression. Also, nearly 25 percent of the trade passing through Singapore's entrepôt port originated in Malaysia, and three-quarters of Singapore's water supply still came from the peninsula. If

Malaysia and Singapore could not agree on peaceful co-existence, then Singapore would be hard hit in every way. At the same time the Tunku realized that if repressive measures were taken against Singapore, Lee Kuan Yew's government would be forced to find friends and trade where it could. This would naturally be with Indonesia, the People's Republic of China, and Communist Russia.

As a result Singapore and Malaysia agreed on continued economic cooperation, and both nations committed themselves to concluding no foreign treaties that would jeopardize the independence or defense of the other. They also agreed on a mutual defense arrangement. In fact, shortly after the separation, Lee sent Singaporean troops to Borneo to aid Malaysia in fighting Indonesian guerrillas.

There was concern in Kuala Lumpur over possible reaction to the expulsion of Singapore among the people of the Borneo states of Sabah and Sarawak. Chinese outnumbered Malays in these states, although the governments were Malay dominated. The governments of Sabah and Sarawak complained that they should have been consulted before such a serious step was undertaken. The Tunku took a hard line. He replied that he did not need to consult East Malaysia for any action the Federal government felt necessary for the common welfare. East Malaysia was the name given to the Borneo states to distinguish them from the peninsular Malay states, which became known as West Malaysia. Sarawak grumbled but accepted the situation, though there was angry talk of secession in Sabah.

The Tunku made a hasty trip to Sabah in late August. There he told Sabah leaders that they lacked sufficient votes in parliament to withdraw legally from the Malaysian union and that he would use force to oppose any attempt by Sabah to leave the union itself. The Malaysian prime minister then forced the resignation of Dato Stephens, the Minister of Sabah Affairs, who was the chief critic of the federal policy.

The Malaysian government, seeking a scapegoat for the dissatisfaction in East Malaysia, blamed the British. The Tunku said that visiting Sabah and Sarawak was like visiting an old British colonial possession. Everyone admitted that this was partly true. Sabah and Sarawak were still underdeveloped and the people untrained in administration. The governments of both states filled the gap with trained British administrators. These administrators were contemptuous of orders from Kuala Lumpur as a general rule, but—probably on direct order from London—were unanimous in discouraging talk of Sabah seceding from Malaysia. Anti-British sentiment in Kuala Lumpur was increased by British Prime Minister Harold Wilson's Labour government, then in power, because it seemed to favor Lee Kuan Yew and the socialistic movement in Singapore.

Lee suddenly announced that he would like to make peace with Indonesia. At the same time the Singaporean prime minister started a definitely anti-American campaign. Lee announced that if the United States tried to move into the political vacuum left by British withdrawal from Southeast Asia, he would open Singapore to Russia for naval bases. Actually, the United States was so deeply involved in Vietnam that she could have done little in Malaysia even if Washington had been inclined to intervene in the Borneo trouble. It was suggested without confirmation that part of Lee's anti-American sentiment came from his belief that the United States was indirectly concerned with the failure of Lee's Malaysia Solidarity Convention through which he hoped to gain political domination of Malaysia. This theory claimed that Lee had been impressed with the way the dominant white race in the United States was giving way under the pressure of militant minorities. He assumed the same thing would happen in Malaysia when he made his militant call for minorities to join him. When this did not happen, Lee developed an unreasoning resentment.

Lee, of course, never revealed the reasons for his actions. There is still another theory that he was never really anti-American, but that anti-Americanism was popular in Southeast Asia. It helped his rapport with Indonesia and with radicals within his own government. Despite his threats to open bases to Russia, his anti-American statements and his definitely leftish leanings, Lee kept a firm grip on communism in Singapore. He understood very well that Singapore's very life as a city and state depended upon the free flow of trade. To this end he announced that Singapore would not align itself with either East or West.

On the domestic front, Lee Kuan Yew echoed the principles

A Nation in Danger

he had put forth in the Solidarity Conference. The Chinese were the majority race in Singapore, but Lee insisted that it was not a Chinese republic—a third China, as one writer called it. Singapore was to be, in Lee's view, the true multi-racial nation that he had envisioned Malaysia to be. To this end he urged everyone to consider himself as a Singaporean rather than a Chinese, Malay, Indian, or European. Kuala Lumpur officials looked upon Lee's actions in this respect as an attempt to show in a model Singaporean community what could have been accomplished in Malaysia if his Malaya Solidarity Convention had been accepted.

At the same time Lee continued to pursue his socialistic ideals. Free trade continued, but citizens were heavily taxed to secure funds for social improvements. Housing has improved and the general standard of living has increased. Businessmen also have been kept happy by trade that has continued to thrive under President Lee Kuan Yew's policy of free trade.

The situation in Borneo (East Malaysia) was a paramount worry to the Tunku and his Kuala Lumpur officials in the days immediately following the separation of Singapore and Malaysia. Sukarno's Confrontation was continuing. Although the British had troops in Borneo to help the Malaysian army, and Singapore had sent its one battalion—all it had—the regular troops were having difficulty stopping the Indonesian guerrillas' hit-and-run attacks across the long frontier. The dissatisfaction in Sabah and Sarawak over the split with Singapore was the major cause of the Tunku's worry. This dissatisfaction could easily be turned to Indonesia's advantage. Sukarno in Indonesia thought the same thing and believed that he would shortly overrun the two Malay states. Then they would be absorbed into Kalimantan (South Borneo).

Before this could come about Sukarno suddenly found himself in trouble. His economic policies, expropriation of foreign businesses which ended foreign investment in Indonesia, and continual war making had brought Indonesia to the brink of bankruptcy. As troubles built up, Sukarno turned more and more to Communist help. Then on the night of September 30, 1965, there was a sudden insurrection in Djakarta, the capital of Indonesia. Pro-Communist members of Sukarno's party attacked

General Nasution, the anti-Communist Armed Forces Chief of Staff. Nasution was wounded, but escaped, although six other army generals were killed. The revolutionary headquarters put out a communiqué saying that the revolt was to prevent army generals, working in "connivance with the United States Central Intelligence Agency," from overthrowing President Sukarno.

The revolt was crushed on October 1 by Lieutenant General Suharto, a hero of the war for independence against the Dutch, who took command when General Nasution was wounded and the Army Chief of Staff slain. The revolt then spread into central Indonesia but was brought under control by October 15. Sukarno issued a communiqué saying he was still in control. (He had been elected President for life in 1962.) However, from that point on the Indonesian army issued the orders. The Communist Party was banned and its offices looted. The government-backed trade union was abolished, and widespread executions of suspected Communist sympathizers were carried on in the Indonesian provinces. Sukarno continued as President, but in March 1966 General Suharto emerged as the army strong man. Sukarno was kept in office as a figurehead for another year and then was dismissed in 1967 when Suharto became acting President. Suharto ended Sukarno's "Crush Malaysia" policy and brought Indonesia back into the United Nations.

The fall of Sukarno was a blessing to Malaysia, ending the Confrontation in Borneo. This in turn eased some of the Tunku's worries about Sabah and Sarawak. It did not, however, solve the more pressing problem of interracial discord. The bitterness among Chinese, Malays, and Indians remained, waiting only for an excuse to explode into violence.

CHAPTER TWELVE

The Kuala Lumpur Riots

THE YEAR 1966 was a good one for Malaysia. The Confrontation ended. Business boomed. The country's balance of payments went on the plus side as exports exceeded imports. Progress was made in opening new lands for agriculture, and a good economic plan was working to develop new industry. Palm oil, for example, proved to be a good money crop that partially offset the fall of rubber prices. On the international front the good news included restoration of diplomatic relations with the Philippines and the possibility of American aid to hasten Malaysia's economic five-year plan.

On the racial front the situation slowly grew worse. Prime Minister Lee Kuan Yew of Singapore had not given up his ambition to dictate Malaysian racial policy despite having been thrown out of the Malaysian union for his previous efforts. The Tunku warned Lee about his continued attacks on the touchy "Malay Rights" question, but Lee ignored the warnings. Though he could not operate directly in Malaysia, Lee had other means to get his message across. A Malayan Indian named Devan Nair registered a new party in Kuala Lumpur which he called the Democratic Action Party. Outwardly there was no connection with Singapore or its controversial prime minister, yet the Democratic Action Party followed the identical multi-racial course set by Lee's PAP party in the days immediately preceding the separation of Singapore and Malaysia.

The year 1966 also saw a new crisis in Sarawak. The Chief Minister, as the state executive was called, bitterly resented interference in Sarawak affairs by the federal government in Kuala Lumpur. The Chief Minister, Dato Ningkan, was an Iban (Sea Dayak) and suspicious of the Malays. In June 1966 Dato Ningkan dismissed his Minister for Communications, who was a Malay, accusing the minister of plotting the Chief Minister's overthrow. The Tunku immediately removed Dato Ningkan as head of the Sarawak branch of the Alliance Party (the Tunku's own party) and demanded his resignation as Sarawak's Chief Minister. Dato Ningkan refused and was ousted. He took his case to the Sarawak Supreme Court, which ruled the ouster illegal. The Tunku then issued a proclamation of emergency and had the federal parliament pass a law changing the state constitution to permit the Chief Minister's removal.

Dato Ningkan denounced the action as a mockery of democracy and claimed his ouster was caused by his refusal to get rid of the British administrators in his state government. The Tunku had denounced the continued use of British in these posts the previous year, saying that a visit to Sarawak was like a visit to pre-Merdeka colonial Borneo. Dato Ningkan claimed that there were no Sarawakans capable of assuming these offices at this time and that the Tunku knew it. The Tunku, Dato charged, wanted the British removed so that Malays from West Malaysia could take the positions. This would accomplish the double purpose of giving the Tunku a more secure grasp on the state government and preventing the Dayaks and other Borneo aborigines from being developed into government administrators. The peninsular Malays intended to use every means to preserve their rights to control the government and all the people of Malaysia.

The racial situation in Malaysia was building up to an explosion. The younger generation of Chinese were not content to remain second-class citizens, as their fathers were. Chinese youth have, in addition to political resentment, a strong sense of racial pride. The Chinese race, they feel, had a great civilization when the Malays still ran naked in the jungles.

This resentment was kept alive by segregation of the two races. Neither had ever gotten to really know the other. Segregation in Malaysia was not forced as it was in the United States or in South Africa, but was the result of mutual desire. Neither race ever wanted to be assimilated into the other. Each had its own background of culture and religion and ideals. And neither wanted to change these. Intermarriage is a traditional way to break down segregation between races living in a single country. This did not happen in Malaysia because of the religious barrier. Muslim Malays usually do not marry outside their religion. The same religious barrier also prevented Malays and Indians from intermarrying. While it is true that Muslim Indians first introduced the religion of Islam to the Malay Peninsula, the bulk of Indians who later migrated to Malaya were Hindus rather than Muslims. This left the races of Malaysia segregated not only physically and politically but also mentally, economically, and spiritually.

Violence finally was provoked by the election of 1969. It was a bitter and hard-fought campaign and gave notice that old values were crumbling. The racial issue was paramount and politicians played it up outrageously. The Tunku's Alliance Party had won almost three-quarters of the votes in the 1965 election. None of the Tunku's opponents thought he could unseat the prime minister. What they were striving for was to capture as many seats as possible in parliament. This would show the strength of the opposition and force the Tunku to be more cooperative. It would also give the opposition a platform from which to build for future expansion, which they hoped would eventually give the opposition control of the government.

The Democratic Action Party claimed to be for all Malaysians but was actually Chinese controlled. It directly challenged the Malayan Chinese Association (MCA) which had cooperated with the Tunku through the Alliance Party. It soon became apparent that the Democratic Action Party (DAP) would draw a considerable number of Chinese votes that had previously gone to the "safe" Malayan Chinese Association candidates. Immediately DAP was attacked both by Tan Siew Sin, MCA chairman, and the Tunku. Tunku Abdul Rahman accused DAP of being inspired by Singapore's Lee Kuan Yew.

"The DAP is anti-Malay," the Tunku charged in an angry election speech. "This party owes its allegiance to a foreign power."

Next the Tunku warned the Chinese that the Alliance Party would not deal with any Chinese organization except MCA, and that MCA was the only organization that could adequately serve Chinese interests. DAP countered with the claim that it was more truly representative of all Malaysia than the Alliance Party, which did not even assimilate its own members, but kept the Malays segregated in the United Malay National Organization, the Chinese in the Malayan Chinese Association, and the Indians in the Malayan Indian Congress. "This proves that the Alliance is race conscious," DAP asserted. "MCA has surrendered Chinese rights to UMNO."

A candidate of Indian extraction said bitterly, "Alliance leaders have said that if we don't like it here we can go back to India or to China. We will not go anywhere. We will stay in Malaysia, the country that we have helped build with our sweat and our blood!"

A Chinese candidate of DAP cried to another election rally: "The Chinese and the Indians joined in the fight for independence because we were promised equality. Where is that equality?"

Tun Razak, the Tunku's deputy prime minister, bluntly told the constituents that if they expected state aid from the federal government, to remember "that we reward support with benevolence. This is no blackmail. This is straight and sincere talk."

The election was held May 10, 1969. The results were a surprise both to the government party and to the opposition. The Tunku's party won as expected, but the opposition parties gained more seats than either side expected. The Alliance Party's eighty-nine West Malaysia seats in parliament were cut to sixty-six. The Malayan Chinese Association had twenty-seven seats previously and the new election cut them to thirteen.

The young Chinese hailed this as a tremendous victory and staged a victory rally and demonstration in the streets of Kuala Lumpur. This increased Malay uneasiness and distrust of the Chinese. The Tunku's UMNO portion of the Alliance Party announced that it would stage its own demonstration to counterbalance the Chinese victory celebration. At the same time Tan

The Kuala Lumpur Riots

Siew Sin, head of MCA, resigned as finance minister in the Tunku's cabinet. He had been given the post—the only one in the cabinet held by a Chinese—as a reward for MCA support of the Alliance Party in the past. When Tan Siew Sin resigned, Tun Razak, deputy prime minister, said, "We told the electorate that if they did not vote MCA, there would be no Chinese representation in the government."

In addition to being the state capital, Kuala Lumpur is also the capital of the state of Sengalor. The state's chief minister (governor) was barricaded in his home by groups of Chinese youths on the morning of May 11. They shouted, "Malays are finished! The Chinese will run the country!"

Two days later Malay youth groups began congregating in Kuala Lumpur. Many came from outside the city and some from outside the states, indicating that they were well organized. They began a demonstration supporting the Tunku's UMNO party, but the demonstration turned into a riot. The Malay youths charged into the streets, attacking Chinese people and their business places and overturning Chinese-owned cars.

"The ferocity of the Malays in the first clashes seems to have surprised everyone," wrote John Slimming, whose book *Malaysia: Death of a Democracy* gives a vivid picture of the wild disorder during the race riots.

In the business section of the capital, Chinese shopkeepers tried to organize a defense of their property. They drove back the Malays at one point and then attacked Malay property in retaliation. This give and take was only temporary, for the Malays quickly regained the initiative, and the fighting spread. The government declared martial law, dispersed troops, and clamped down a curfew. None of these measures did any good. The violence continued through the night.

The next day—Wednesday—was comparatively quiet, but the seething fury was still there waiting for a new chance to break loose again. Soldiers patrolled the city with orders to shoot to kill. Fires were still burning in the city and many of the dead bodies had not been picked up. The curfew was enforced rigidly against the Chinese, keeping them indoors, but Malays continued to roam the streets.

The government seemed afraid to crack down on the Malays.

And the Tunku later claimed that he spent Wednesday morning alternately praying and weeping. However, late Wednesday the Tunku went on the radio to read a proclamation putting the country in a state of emergency. He bitterly blamed the disturbances on Communist elements, claiming that the terrorists who fought to take over Malaya after World War II were back to renew their struggle. The proclamation of emergency, first drawn up to cover the state of Sengalor in which the capital Kuala Lumpur was situated, was expanded to include the entire nation. It also suspended the general elections which had not yet been held in Sabah and Sarawak. This last stipulation created additional bitterness in Borneo against the central government. After one day of comparative quiet, violence was renewed on Thursday night when rampaging mobs of Malays—joined in many cases by soldiers—began looting and burning Chinese homes. By the next morning more than five thousand Chinese were homeless and huddled fearfully in refugee centers.

The government was placed under a National Operations Council headed by Deputy Prime Minister Tun Razak, who was given dictatorial powers. Tun Razak hastened to announce that he was still responsible to the Tunku and would form an emergency council to aid in restoring order. This council, he said, would be multi-racial. However, the only Chinese included in the Council was Tan Siew Sin, the head of the Malayan Chinese Association which so many Chinese voters had repudiated in the ill-fated election that sparked the rioting.

The curfew was continued for the rest of the month of May, and heavy press censorship was in force. The government was especially bitter toward the foreign press, claiming that the riots had been blown out of proportion by correspondents. Officially the Tunku's government said that only 176 persons had been killed, while the correspondents' estimates ranged from 800 to more than a thousand. Both the American *Time* and *Newsweek* magazines were banned for the stories they carried on the riots and so were such famous papers as the *London Times*. Copies of *The Times* were smuggled into Kuala Lumpur and sold for as much as M$20. (A Malaysian dollar at the time was worth 33 cents U.S.)

Both the Tunku and Tun Razak continued to hammer away

at the claim that the riots were Communist inspired. This did not help the situation since the average Malay, remembering the long Communist campaign following World War II, looked upon all Chinese as Communist sympathizers. So the situation settled into an uneasy truce. The Malays, mindful of the large number of Chinese in their country, expected a Chinese retaliation. The Chinese in turn were fearful of a repetition of the bloody May riots and knew from bitter experience that they could not count on police or army protection if the violence was renewed.

Both the Tunku and Tun Razak insisted that the trouble was over and tried to maintain the fiction that the disturbance had not been as serious as reports indicated. One Malay official compared the outburst of violence with the ancient Malay custom of "running amok." Running amok among the Malays was noted by early British writers, and it was a great favorite with pulp fiction writers of adventure stories set in the East. Running amok has been described as the build-up of frustration and anger in the usually peaceful and easygoing Malay until he reaches the point where his emotions explode. Then he grabs a *parang* (sword) and runs wildly down the street, killing and slashing everyone in his path, friend or foe.

Running amok among individual Malays was never stamped out by the British in their long years of judicial administration, because like murder, running amok is caused by passions that overbalance the victim's mind and judgment. However, prompt application of the hangman's rope for those who ran amok greatly reduced its frequency in early day Singapore and Penang. A peculiar characteristic of those running amok was that if they were lucky enough to escape British justice, it was very rare that the perpetrator ever repeated his crime. Those who were caught never seemed to resent their punishment but took it as their just fate. Charles Buckley quoted the story told by one British judge who said that he wanted to be sure that the condemned man understood why he was being executed. The judge felt that many of those he punished never really understood, for their ideas of justice were different from British ideas. So he gave a long discourse and then told the interpreter to pass it along to the prisoner. The interpreter spoke two sentences and the prisoner nodded his head as if satisfied. "Did you tell him *all* I said?" inquired the judge. "Oh, yes, *tuan*," the interpreter replied smiling. "You said he's wrong, he hangs. I told him. He understands."

Though the rioters behaved like men running amok during the violence, there is evidence that their behavior was not spontaneous and that men were brought in from the outlying sections in deliberate anticipation of trouble designed "to teach the Chinese a lesson." It also varied from the traditional "running amok" in that the trouble broke out again. The second explosion was not as violent as the first and was directed against the Indians, Malaysia's second largest minority after the Chinese. The new trouble began on the night of June 28, 1969 and raged through the night. By morning fifteen Indians were dead and about eighty were in refugee camps after their homes had been burned. Following the attack on the Indians, the rioters then turned and burned several Chinese homes.

As could be expected, the Kuala Lumpur riots shocked Singapore, then 75 percent Chinese and naturally in sympathy with the beleaguered Chinese in Kuala Lumpur. Some Chinese youth gangs attempted to retaliate against Malays in Singapore but were quickly controlled by the anxious government. Lee Kuan Yew immediately formed multi-racial security groups to patrol the city. The idea of having the security forces composed of Chinese, Malays, and Indians was to prevent a situation occurring as in Kuala Lumpur where Malay soldiers and the police aided their own race instead of protecting the Chinese victims of the riot. Singapore had suffered from bitter race riots in 1964 and the government was determined that they would not happen again.

There was no more violence in Kuala Lumpur, but the bitterness and hatred remained. Racial antagonism remained at a high pitch. Tun Razak did not feel safe in relaxing government by decree and the parliament remained suspended until 1970.

One of the government's first moves to lessen the tension was to require all schools to convert to teaching only in the Malay language. Previously both English and Chinese were used in the elementary schools, for many Chinese and Indian children could not speak Malay. The reason for requiring all future teaching to be done in Malay was, the government said, to give all races a feeling of belonging to Malaysia. This order applied only to public schools, and many Chinese and Indians were forced to send their children to private schools because they did not speak enough Malay to continue their studies. As a result, this order increased minority bitterness instead of lessening it, as the government claimed it was designed to do.

The Chinese and Indians insisted that the language order was another government effort to humiliate them and to drive their children out of government-supported schools, increasing segregation. They also complained that the government housing program was designed to drive minorities out of the capital. In one case the government uprooted several thousand Chinese from slum areas as part of a low-cost housing program. The shanties occupied by the poorer class Chinese were destroyed, but the new houses were never built. Then in mid-1970 the funds allocated to the low-income units were cut off.

The most significant event of 1970 was the resignation of Tunku Abdul Rahman as prime minister. The resignation closed twenty years of political domination by the Tunku. He had taken over as leader of the United Malays National Organization in 1951 and in 1955 he became Chief Minister of Malaya under the British. Two years later he became prime minister when Malaya achieved full independence. He continued as prime minister through three general elections, but after the riots he passed the job, if not the title, to his deputy Tun Abdul Razak, who directed the government through emergency decree.

The Tunku had come under increasing fire from his Malay constituents in the two years between the riots and his resignation. The government's precarious position was summed up by John Slimming in this way: "The immediate prospects for multi-racial cooperation are bleak. The present UMNO leaders cannot risk offending the Malays for fear of widening the rift within their own party."

Malay youth particularly refused to be placated. At one point 1,500 demonstrated at the Malaya University campus, accusing the Tunku of being pro-British. Then a University professor published an inflammatory pamphlet which the government

Tunku Abdul Rahman, architect of the Malaysian nation. He is wearing the tengkolok, *the traditional Malay headgear, in this official Malaysian government photograph.*

quickly banned. The pamphlet accused the prime minister of "always giving in to the Chinese . . . Our present enemies are not only the Chinese and the Indians, but also the Americans, British, and Australians. In their discussions they have clearly sided with the Indians and the Chinese."

This continued criticism finally led to the Tunku's resignation in 1971. His successor, Tun Abdul Razak, had always been the Tunku's deputy and was looked upon almost as the Tunku's adopted son. The two were very close. As a result, no one expects the change to make any difference in government policy, since Tun Razak has been prime minister in all but name since the formation of the emergency National Operations Council during the 1969 riots.

Bandar Street in Kuala Lumpur, the nation's capital, is a mixture of Chinese-type shops and high-rise financial structures.

CHAPTER THIRTEEN

Malaysia Today

MALAYSIA today is a split world. There is the world of the cities and the world of the back country. Traditionally the Malay people have not been town dwellers. From historic times the towns were reserved for the ruling class and those who supported them. The usual Malay river or port town consisted of a central area where the ruling class lived and conducted government business. Around this nucleus different trading groups separated according to race and nationality and built their own settlements. This came about because the rajahs and the sultans were very much engaged in trade and in controlling trade. The average Malay cared little for business, and as a result the average Malay city and town had a predominantly higher foreign population.

This is still true today. The capital city of Kuala Lumpur has 760,000 people spread over its 37 square miles of territory. The government estimates that 61 percent of these are Chinese, 17 percent are Indians, 15 percent are Malays, and other peoples, including Europeans, make up the remaining 7 percent. The Chinese control the major portion of the city's industry and business. The civil servants, running the government and city, are mainly Malays because of the constitutional restrictions on employing non-Malays.

In December 1971 the government went a step further in its "Malaysia for Malays" program. It ordered the employment of Malays in middle management of private business, somewhat in the same manner that the United States has forced government contractors to employ a larger number of minority race members. Arshad Ayub of the Mara Institute of Technology in Kuala Lumpur blamed the imbalance on Chinese employers' prejudice against the Malays.

"The racial imbalance was doubtless initially caused by colonial policy," he said. "But the colonial fox is dead, and it is high time we stop blaming everything on him. The notion that the Malay is lazy and incapable is outmoded, but there are still remnants of the prejudice against employing him.

"If the Malays are backward, pessimistic, fatalistic, and not competitive enough, it is the duty of the public and the private sectors to help change their values," he added.

Speaking for the government at a management meeting in Kuala Lumpur on December 29, 1971, Musa Hitam, a member of parliament, said soothingly, "Speaking as a politician I should like to point out that the philosophy of Malay rights and privileges is just a temporary measure to achieve a certain aim. This aim—a restructuring of society—will be fully achieved only when every Malay can proudly say, 'I got this job not because I am a Malay, but because I am the best qualified of the applicants. I won it in open competition.' "

Musa Hitam acknowledged that the government measure enforcing the employment of a larger number of Malays in middle management was unfortunate. "But it is necessary," he added, acknowledging that employment of untrained Malays in these positions would cause some business setbacks. "But this," he said, "will be more than made up for by the long-term profit brought about by the stability and contentment of the population."

Chinese youth in turn want to know how "contentment of the population" can be brought about when scarce jobs are set aside for only 15 percent of the city's population. They also wonder what good are education and experience when the government forces private employers to hire Malays simply because they are Malays.

Even Malay college graduates are finding that jobs are hard to get. When the country began developing there was a shortage of engineers, and young people rushed to get into engineering professions. Unfortunately job opportunities are limited in these fields, and there are few openings for new graduates today. While the economy continues to expand, it is not doing so at a fast enough rate to take care of all graduates. This frightens Chinese and Indian youth. They fear that the "Malaysia for the Malays" policy will eventually restrict them to common labor jobs.

The government could not have taken action to force business and industry to employ Malays in preference to other races if it had not felt secure. The election of 1969 shook the Alliance Party, although the party retained power. Since that time two of the new political parties that drew votes from the Alliance have broken up because of internal bickering. The Malayan Chinese Association, which lost so many seats to dissident Chinese, has also made a comeback. Its leader, Tan Siew Sin, again holds the important finance minister portfolio in the national government. (The only important post held by a Chinese.)

Outwardly Kuala Lumpur show little sign of the racial unrest. In structure it is a hodge-podge of old Malaya and new Malaysia. The Parliament Building is a magnificent example of modern architecture. New hotels, office buildings, and financial buildings are also adding a more modern atmosphere to the city. But these rub shoulders with architecture that looks like something out of the *Arabian Nights*. Much of the Moorish architecture is a British heritage. The British at one time tried to build all new public buildings in Moorish style to generate favor with the Islamic Malays. Thus the railroad station in Kuala Lumpur is mistaken for a sultan's palace by visitors until informed otherwise. The Chinese section of the city resembles Taipei and Hong Kong.

From the air the city can be seen sprawling in a valley formed by hills on three sides. The Klang and Gombak rivers cut into the city and meet at the exact center to form a single channel that flows on to the sea. A Moorish-type mosque is situated at the confluence of the rivers, occupying the exact spot where the first settlements were made in Kuala Lumpur. The beautiful

The first settlement in Kuala Lumpur was made here where the Klang and Gombak rivers meet. An Arabian-Nights–type mosque now occupies the spot where the city began 111 years ago. Kuala Lumpur takes its name from Malay words meaning "muddy river mouth."

name (pronounced koo-AH-la lum-POOR) translates as "Muddy River Mouth" and refers to the dirty condition of the water where the two rivers come together.

The city was founded to exploit tin deposits found in the area. Previously tin was mined principally in Perak state, but in 1830 the local sultan began prospecting for new deposits. This went on for twenty-seven years before the sultan's nephew and two Chinese businessmen found rich tin deposits near where the Klang and Gombak rivers meet. The first miners died of malaria and a new group was sent in by the sultan. After the mine was well started, two Chinese traders, Hiu Siew and Ah Sze Keledek, started a small trading post at the Muddy River Mouth in 1859. The settlement grew rapidly and then for several years was gripped by a struggle between two Chinese miners' secret societies. In 1880 the Sengalor capital was moved to this location and Sir Frank Swettenham became British resident.

Swettenham viewed the dirty, unhealthy palm-thatch village as a disgrace for a state capital. He began a campaign to improve the city, finally getting the Malay government, the British administration in Singapore and local businessmen to cooperate. He gradually had the town torn down block by block and replaced with brick and stucco structures. From that time Kuala Lumpur continued to expand as new industries were opened in the regions about it. From a population of 4,000 in 1886 when Swettenham's renovation program started, the number of inhabitants increased to 25,000 by 1896.

One of the showplaces of modern Malaysia is Petaling Jaya, a "satellite town," as the Malays say. Americans would call it an industrial suburb of the capital. Located seven miles from the center of Kuala Lumpur, Petaling Jaya is a planned industrial community which provides a place for industrial development and homes for those who work for the companies located there. The homes and townhouse-style apartments are upper middle class, beautifully designed and equal to homes in the $25-to-$35,000 bracket in the United States. Businesses in Petaling Jaya range from tire manufacturing to Japanese noodles. The noodle business is very good, so much so that the company is planning a second factory. Most of the companies are branches of German, British, and Chinese firms, but in the shopping

The National Mosque in Kuala Lumpur is a modernized version of the traditional Islamic place of worship.

A Malay kampong in a forest. The dwelling in the foreground is raised off the ground in the Malay tradition, but the storage warehouse in the center sits directly on the ground.

Even with plentiful land available, Malays prefer to live on the water's edge. They consider their stilt-supported homes cooler and more sanitary. This is a fishing village on an island in the Straits of Malacca.

center there is an American representative: Colonel Sanders' Kentucky Fried Chicken.

Other principal Malaysia cities are smaller than Kuala Lumpur. Georgetown, the capital of Penang Island, has 400,000 people and is important as a free port where tourist ships stop. Few call the city by its name, but generally refer to it as "Penang," which is actually the name of the island. Malacca, once the greatest city in Malaya, is now reduced to 70,000 people. Seremban, capital of Negri Sembilan state, has 130,000 inhabitants, and Ipoh, capital of Perak, has 135,000.

Beyond the cities, life goes on much as it has for centuries. The *kampong* is the social unit. Kampong means village. It is ruled by a headman who is elected by the villagers. Those who live in the village are usually related and their ancestry is traced matrilineally back to a common grandmother. The houses, always built on stilts, are clustered together. The villagers walk to their fields or fishing piers, depending on how they make their living. In the mountainous back country some aborigine tribes still live by hunting or "slash and burn" agriculture, which means they clear land with fire and ax, farm until the soil is exhausted, and then move on to a new location.

Customs vary within individual villages, tribes, and clans. Thus it is difficult to pinpoint any one custom and say that it is universal. Often a custom partakes of a smattering of different cultures. A Malay wedding is a double affair, including both a traditional ceremony based on Hinduism and a Muslim ceremony based upon the national religion. The traditional Hindu-style wedding includes binding the bride and groom together with a bridal cord. The Muslim part of the wedding does not permit the bride's presence. In this ceremony the bridegroom and the girl's father or representative appear before a religious official. After prayer, the father offers the bride in marriage in exchange for a previously agreed marriage settlement. The groom accepts. The amount of money is usually small and becomes the property of the bride.

The combined ceremonies—Malay traditional and Muslim—are required for all Malays. The Muslim ceremony is required by the national religion, but it is not considered sufficient and no couple is permitted to live together until they also go through the traditional ceremony. This, however, applies only to a woman's first marriage. If she divorces and marries again the Muslim ceremony only is required. Divorce is very common —perhaps because first marriages are family-arranged affairs. One source claims that there is one divorce for every two marriages today. Divorce is considered as normal as marriage, and there is no social stigma attached to it.

Children are welcome in Malay families, and girls are cherished as much as boys—in contrast to the Chinese. In fact, Malay families often prefer girls because they believe that daughters take better care of elderly parents than sons do.

The rural communities also keep alive the traditional *wayang kulit* or shadow play which has its counterpart in plays of Cambodia and Java. In practice the operator sits behind a sheet and operates a jointed flat figure of the characters. A light behind him throws the shadow of the figure on the screen. The plays depict scenes from the *Ramayana,* the Indian epic of Prince Rama's search for his stolen wife, Sita; tales of Hang Tuah, the great Malaccan period hero; and stories from the *Malay Annals.* The *Ramayana* is popular in all countries that have been touched by Hindu culture, but the Hang Tuah and *Malay Annals* plays are purely Malay.

Another Malay tradition seen at many weddings as part of the entertainment and more often performed for tourists is *Bersilat* or the art of Malayan self-defense. In its exhibition form (called *Silat Pulat*) it more closely resembles a sword-fight dance between two participants. It usually ends with one dancer losing his weapon and then overcoming his opponent despite the other's sword. A more deadly form, *Silat Buah,* is reserved for serious fighting. Teachers of *Silat Buah* have their own secret methods which they pass along to their students.

Dancing is also popular with Malay people. Many of the folk dances preserve pre-Islamic customs and beliefs that are decidedly at odds with orthodox Mohammedanism. The Saucer Dance retains the rituals for offering food to spirits of the woods. The Rice Harvest Dance is probably older than Hinduism in Malaya which goes back to the first century A.D. It was originally danced to placate the spirits of the rice field and ensure a bountiful harvest. The Handkerchief Dance has a more

A Malay miss has put flowers in her hair and donned the traditional brocade costume to participate in a Malay folk dance.

basic appeal. The weaving dancer waves a handkerchief which symbolically is wet with tears for a faithless lover. However, the most popular Malay folk dance is the *Ronggeng,* which is danced to a catchy tune (said to be of Portuguese origin) played by flute and drum. It is danced by a man and woman who move closely together but are not permitted to touch. The exact steps and movements vary in different localities, although the music remains the same.

Radio, television and films are also popular in today's Malaysia. Radio is a late comer. Originally a few ham operators represented the only radio in the country. The first actual station was set up by the government in Kuala Lumpur in 1939. After World War II the government organized Radio Malaya primarily as a propaganda vehicle during the twelve-year emergency when the country was fighting Chan Peng's Chinese guerrillas. Today the radio system has expanded until its domestic service branch broadcasts 420 hours a week in Malay, English, Hindi, and Chinese. There are three networks so that there can be simultaneous broadcasts of entertainment, information, and education.

Television service began in December 1963 and went commercial in 1965. There are now eleven transmitters in Malaysia that cover West Malaysia, Singapore, and part of Sumatra. Plans are underway to extend TV facilities to the Borneo states. There are an estimated 165,000 TV sets in operation as compared with 479,164 licensed radio receivers.

CHAPTER FOURTEEN

Looking to a Troubled Tomorrow

MALAYSIA has made definite economic progress in her fight to escape from complete dependence on tin and rubber to keep the country alive. At the present time there are over 200 separate articles being manufactured in the country and more are in the planning stage. Social progress is making some headway. The vigorous low-cost housing program, interrupted for a while after the riots, is again underway. Squatters, dispossessed from their shanties to make room for fifteen-story apartment houses, have been given rooms in the buildings. They do not all look upon this as a blessing from a benevolent government.

"For a man and his wife and maybe one or two children," one resident reported, "they are fine. But when a family of six such as I have lives in these apartments there is just not room enough.

"And," he added in a sorrowful tone that bespoke experience, "there are no elevators in these low-cost dwellings. If one has an apartment on the fifteenth floor, it is a hard, hard climb at the end of a long working day. Maybe this is a government plot to keep everyone home, for one is not about to climb down and back up again until he has to leave for work again in the morning!"

However, despite progress economically and socially, Malaysia's two basic conflicts—communism and race—remain. Either of them is sufficient to destroy the young nation in the years ahead. Actually the two conflicts are tied together in a way. Racism and the Malays' fear of losing control of their government are working to the benefit of communism through alienation of young Chinese who look to communism to free them from Malay domination. The Malaysian government realizes this but is powerless to do anything about it. The temper of the Malay people is such that if the government took any other stand than its "Malaysia for Malays" policy, the people would destroy the government. In a review of this situation, J. M. Gullick (in the British *World Studies Series*) said, "Only the withering away of communal loyalties and the growth of a new national consciousness can eliminate the government's dilemma. Such a change may be achieved in time, but it will require a long and untroubled period of evolution for its full flowering." Gullick wrote this before the bloody race riots of 1969 made the "withering away of communal loyalties" more remote than ever.

The Communists, of course, are aware of the situation and are naturally going to make the most of it. The *Asian,* one of the leading newspapers in the Far East, reported in its January 2, 1972 issue: "Chan Peng's Malayan Communist Party is working hard to rebuild the mass support infrastructure destroyed during the 1948–1960 emergency. There is disturbing evidence of Communist penetration among the Chinese population of Perak and Kedah."

Then, referring to the Borneo states, the paper said, "The situation in Sarawak gives more immediate cause for concern . . . The Communists are strongly entrenched in the Third Division and there is increasing evidence that they are winning vital Dayak support."

Also, as the war in Vietnam began de-escalating in 1970, there was renewed Chinese Communist guerrilla activity along the Malaysia-Thailand border. Communists hailed it as a renewal of the "long war"—that is, the twelve-year struggle that followed World War II. This border fighting increased slightly during 1971 but is still not a distinct threat.

The main problem is still racial strife. The official government position is that the situation is correcting itself, but outside of government circles neither the Malays nor the Chinese believe that any progress has been made.

"If the Chinese were less numerous, integration would be possible," one said. "Nothing can ever be done now. Malaysia lost a tremendous asset when she lost Singapore. But what choice did she have? Lee Kuan Yew is a very brilliant and forceful man. If he had remained in Malaysia he would have been like the freezing camel in the Arab fable. You remember that the kind-hearted Arab let the camel stick his nose into the Arab's tent and before long the camel was in the tent and the poor Arab was out in the cold. So it would be with us Malays if Lee Kuan Yew and Singapore had remained in the Malay union."

In Singapore Lee Kuan Yew has the problem of trying to provide jobs and a decent living standard for his crowded city-state. In addition to Singapore Island, he also governs several small islands in the vicinity. Today they are inhabited primarily by fishermen, but they figure strongly in Lee's plans. These plans for the future center on developing new industry to partially free Singapore from complete dependence upon trade and shipping to maintain the nation's economy. In doing so, he has been working with a British firm on the possibility of establishing an aircraft assembly plant in Singapore. He is also exploring the possibility of bringing in some heavy industry. At the same time he is working hard to preserve Singapore as the number one port in Southeast Asia and the fourth largest port in the world. The $50,000,000 improvement to Port Swettenham, twenty miles from Kuala Lumpur, is drawing off some of the entrepôt trade that once went through Singapore. And the recent devaluation of the United States dollar caused shipping lines serving Singapore to boost their rates. This will increase costs in Singapore, threatening business. Lee Kuan Yew retaliated by opening negotiations with the People's Republic of China whereby ten Chinese freighters would be placed on the Singapore-Europe run. Freight could be shipped on these vessels 20 percent cheaper than by ships belonging to the Far East Freight Conference, an organization of shipping companies.

The possibility of opening Singapore to additional Chinese ships is not an indication that Lee Kuan Yew is relaxing

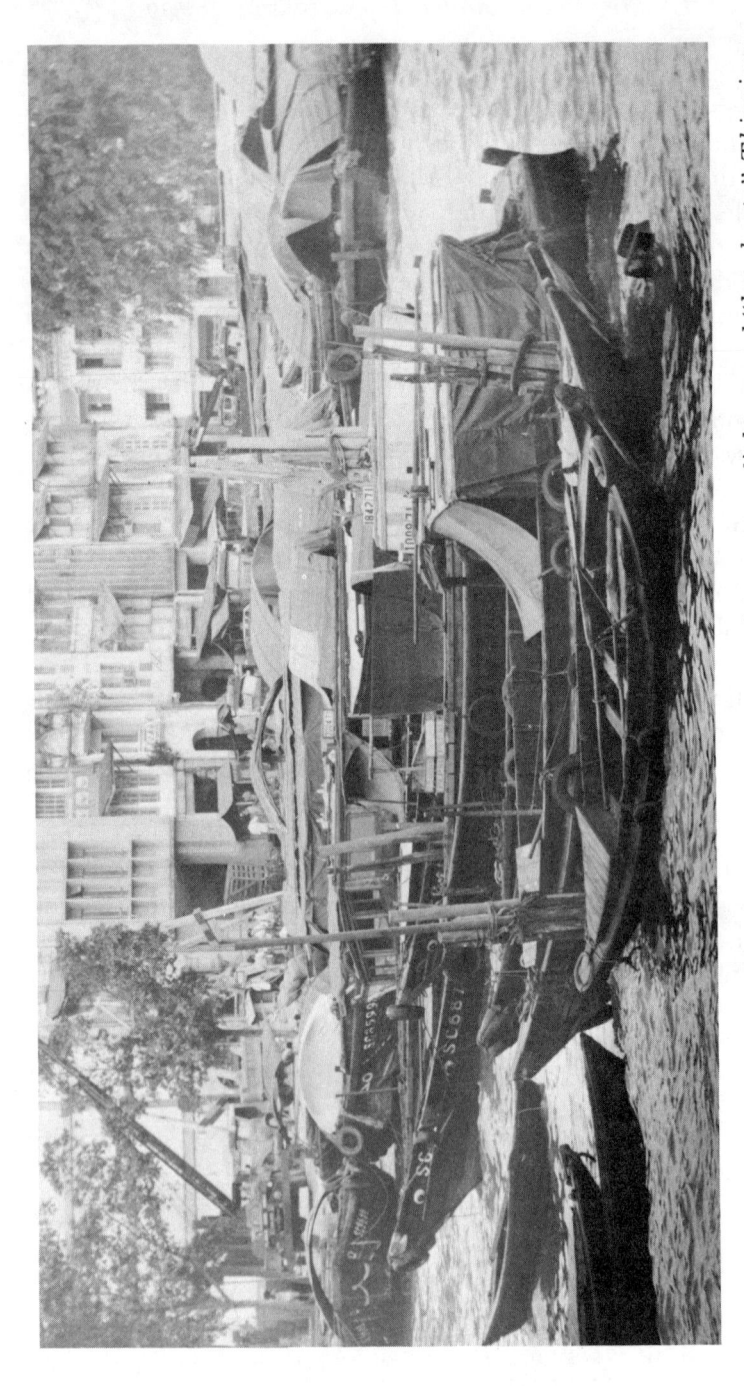

In the early morning mists the Singapore River is jammed with sampans, lighters, and "bumboats." This view looks toward the west bank. This area was originally swamp, but Raffles ordered a hill torn down for dirt to use in reclaiming it.

his firm grip on Communist expansion in Singapore. Although he was originally assumed to be a Communist sympathizer, no one believes this today. He is strictly pro-Singaporean and nothing else. Lee made his position very clear in his strong clampdown on Communist demonstrations in his city. His firmness is shown in a news story appearing in the Singapore *New Nation*, December 31, 1971 issue. Two political prisoners, Kia Ba Ba, twenty-three, and Lim Joo Suan, twenty-two, were released from prison after serving four and two years respectively.

The paper said: "Kia, a former member of a secret Communist study cell in Yock Eng High School, was detained on November 10, 1968—four days after taking part in an illegal demonstration during which a bus was burned.

"He said he now realizes that illegal demonstrations, burning buses and damaging traffic lights were 'not only senseless but also against the interests of the nation and the people.'

"Lim, a former [Communist group] cadre member, took part in a number of illegal demonstrations . . . before he was detained in June of last year.

"He said he now realizes that the Communists were using him to carry out their 'nefarious acts,' and he is determined to sever relations with them."

Apparently Singaporeans do not feel that a four-year sentence for a nineteen-year-old who burns buses is excessive. One who was questioned about it smiled thinly and said, "Perhaps Americans might consider such a sentence for so young a person as being harsh. However, I notice that demonstrations and destruction of public property have stopped in Lee Kuan Yew's Singapore. Has it done the same in the United States?"

While many of Lee Kuan Yew's policies are criticized in Singapore, there is no criticism of the prime minister as a man. He is generally regarded as extremely honest and as running a government as free from corruption as any in the world. All agree that he is definitely for the welfare of the people as a *whole*. This naturally brings him into conflict with various groups interested in their own gain. For these Lee cares nothing if they stand in the way of his master plan for developing Singapore to take care of the people of the future. Private property and estates are subject to government takeover under

The National Parliament Building in Kuala Lumpur, seat of the Malaysian government.

the right of eminent domain at any time Lee feels the land could be used more profitably for housing projects, parks, or public use. The owners, of course, are paid for the land, but resent losing valuable property which cannot be replaced on the small island.

This attitude applies just as surely to groups one would think Lee would favor for political reasons. In December 1971 a group of Hakka Chinese called on the prime minister after all but 11 acres of their 142-acre cemetery was taken for a public use. If they couldn't keep their original acreage, they asked for an equal amount of land in another location. Although Lee knew very well how the Chinese venerate their dead and that his own grandfather was buried in the Hakka cemetery, the prime minister refused. He told the group they could keep only the 11 acres as a memorial to their ancestors. Then he summed up the entire philosophy of his government in adding: "You have done well by the dead, but we as the government must do our best for the living."

Bibliography

Allen, Richard, *Malaysia Prospect and Retrospect,* London, 1968
Arasaratnam, Sinnappah, *Indians in Malaysia,* Bombay, 1970
Buckley, Charles B., *Anecdotal History of Old Singapore,* reprinted Kuala Lumpur, 1970
Cameron, John, *Our Tropical Possessions in Malayan India,* reprinted Kuala Lumpur, 1965
Gullick, J. M. *Malaysia and Its Neighbors,* New York, 1967
Journal of the Royal Asiatic Society, Malaysia Branch, London, 1907–1909
Kennedy, J., *A History of Malaysia A. D. 1400–1959,* London, 1967
Miller, Harry, *A Short History of Malaysia,* New York, 1965
Owen, Frank, *The Fall of Singapore,* London, 1960
Roff, William R., *Origins of Malay Nationalism,* New Haven, 1967
Slimming, John, *Malaysia, Death of a Democracy,* London, 1964
Swettenham, Frank, *Stories and Sketches,* reprinted Kuala Lumpur, 1967
Tweedie, M. W. F., *Prehistoric Malaya,* Singapore, 1955

Periodicals and Newspapers

The Asian, Singapore
The New Nation, Singapore
Newsweek, New York
The Straits Times (Malaysia Edition)
The Straits Times (Singapore Edition)
Time magazine, New York

INDEX

Abdul Rahman, Sultan, 26, 28
Abdul Rahman (the Tunku), *122;* new political leader, 85; independent federation, 86; unification with Singapore, 88–90, 92–3; relations with Indonesia, 95, 103–4; Brunei oil royalties, 96; proposed nation of Malaysia, 98–100; withdrawal of Singapore, 107–8; after Singapore leaves Malaysia, 108–9, 111–13; ouster of Dato Ningkan, 114; 1969 election, 115–16; riots in Kuala Lumpur, 118–19; resigns, 121, 123
Abdul Razak, Tun, 107, 116–21, 123
Abdullah, Munshi, 24, 26, 29–31, 34–5
Abdullah, Sultan, 56, 60
Aborigines, 3–4; in Borneo, 41, 114; legends, 62–3
Acheh, 15, 16
Agriculture, 64–5, 113, 133
Ah Sze Keledek, 129
Alabama (ship), 69
Ala'uddin, Sultan, 12, 13
Alliance Party, 104, 114–17, 127
Amherst, Lord, 39
Amok, 119
Anglo-Dutch Treaty (1824), 36, 37

Arabs, 8
"Asia for Asians" proposal, 77
Asian, 138
Australia, 71, 74–5, 84
Ayub, Arshad, 126
Ayuthia, 8
Azahari, Sheikh A. M., 94, 97

Badang (legendary hero), 32
Batim (Malay Adam), 62
Belcher, Sir Edward, 47
Bencoolen, 22, 27, 28, 33, 36
Bersilat, 134
Birch, James, 61; as Resident, 57–60; murder, 60
Borneo, ix, i, 2, 18, 35, 65, 71, 90, 136; history, 40–2; Indonesian guerrillas in, 109, 111, 112; *see also* North Borneo
Bridge on the River Kwai, 77
British Commonwealth of Nations, 83, 93
British East India Company, 16, 17, 20, 38, 93; in India, 16–17, 36–7, 59; China trade, 18–19; and Raffles, 21, 22, 30, 35; James Brooke in, 40; decline, 48
British North Borneo Chartered Company, 55, 95
Brooke, Sir Charles, 54–5
Brooke, Sir James, 38, 49, 59, 77; background, 39–40; negotia-

145

Brooke, Sir James (cont.)
    tions with Rajah Muda, 43–6;
    faces revolt, 53–4; illegitimate
    son, 54; death, 54
Brunei: Malays settle, 42; James
    Brooke in, 43, 45–7, 54–5; oil,
    77, 93, 96; proposed as part of
    Malaysia, 90, 92–7; Azahari
    revolt, 94–5, 97
Buckley, Charles B., 21–4, 28, 35,
    51, 52, 119
Buddhism, 50
Bugis, 16, 19
Bulkiah, Sultan: see Nakhoda
    Ragam
Burma, 1, 2, 4, 19, 39, 59; in
    World War II, 74–5, 77;
    independence, 83
Burma Road, 74

Cambodia, 7, 67–8
Cameron, John, 13, 32, 52, 61–2
Canada, 71
Canton, 70
Catholicism, 52–3
Caves, 6; cave dwellers, 5; cave
    paintings in Borneo, 41
Cebu, Sultan of, 42
Celebes, 16
Ceylon, 65
Chan Peng, 86, 136, 138
Cheng Ho, Admiral, 8, 11
Chiang Kai-shek, 72, 74, 76, 81
China: trade, 1, 2, 5, 8, 16–19, 48,
    69, 139; immigrants from, 5,
    49, 68–9; protects Malacca, 8–
    11; opium, 19–20; Borneo
    records, 41; war with Japan,
    70, 72, 74, 76
China, Communist, 81, 102, 109,
    139
Chinese in Malaya, 81, 82, 85, 90;

during Japanese occupation,
    76, 79
Chinese in Malaysia: racism
    against, x–xi, 49, 105–7, 112,
    114, 121, 123, 138–9; political
    power, 104–7, 109, 114–16, 118,
    125; Kuala Lumpur riots, 116–
    20; employment, 126–7
Chinese in North Borneo, 77
Chinese secret societies, 50, 52,
    53, 55–6, 78, 105, 129
Chinese in Singapore, 29, 33, 98,
    104–6, 111, 120, 121, 143
Chulalongkorn, King of Siam, 68
Churchill, Winston, 71, 73–5, 80
Clarke, Sir Andrew, 55–7, 61
Clive, Robert (Clive of India), 17
Cobbold Commission, 93–4
Coffee, 64–5
Coleman, John, 63–4, 69
Colonialism, 14, 83, 93
Communism: attracts Chinese in
    Malaysia, x, 78, 138; postwar
    activities, 83–4, 93; in Singa-
    pore, 86–90, 110, 141; in Peo-
    ple's Action Party, 87–9; in
    Indonesia, 104, 111–12; riots in
    Malaysia, 118–19; see also
    Malayan Communist Party
Conference of Rulers, 82
"Co-Prosperity Sphere," 72–3
Coral Sea, Battle of, 78
Cotton, 69
Crawfurd, John, 34–6
Crime, 80, 84; in Singapore, 52–3,
    55, 119
Customs and traditions, 133–4,
    136

D'Albuquerque, Alfonso, 13–14
Dancing, folk, 134–6

Index

Dayaks, 4, 114; in Borneo, 41–4, 47
Democratic Action Party (DAP), 113, 115, 116
Dent, Alfred, 54, 95
De Sequeira, Captain, 13, 14
Deva Shah, 11
Djakarta, 20
Dobby, E. H. G., 2
Drake, Sir Francis, 15
Dutch East India Company, 16
Dutch in Malaya: *see* Netherlands

East India Company: *see* British East India Company; Dutch East India Company
East Malaysia, 1, 3, 109, 111
Economic conditions, 129, 137, 139
Economic cooperation, 109; Japanese plan for Far East, 72–3
Economic depression, 70, 77
Economics controlled by Chinese, x, 49, 106, 107, 125
Education, 121
Elizabeth II, Queen, 85–6
Employment, 126–7
Entrepot trade, 7, 10, 77; *see also* Trade

Fame (ship), 35
Farquhar, William, 28, 34; helps found Singapore, 22, 27; trouble with Raffles, 27, 29, 30, 32–3
Federation of Malaya: *see* Malaya, Federation of
Flint, Raffles, 30
Folklore: *see* Legends
Food shortage, 80–1

Foreign Correspondents' Association of Southeast Asia, 92
France, 19, 59, 65; Revolution, 20; in Indochina, 59, 67–8, 83; in World War II, 70, 72
Free Press (Singapore), 51–3
Funan, 7

George, Reuben, 54
Georgetown, 133
Germany, 55, 58, 59, 70, 78
Ghee Hin Society, 56
Gloucester, Duke of, 85–6
Goa, Portuguese in, 14
Gombak River, 127–9
Goode, Sir William, 87
Goodyear, Charles, 65
Great Britain: military aid, ix, 86; in India, 16–17; trade, 17–20; in Penang, 20–1; relations with Netherlands, 20, 22–4, 28, 35–7, 59; Raffles in Singapore, 22–4, 26–8; Lubuan Island ceded to, 47, 53–4; Residencies in Malaya, 57–8; in Perak, 59–61; Malaya Federation plan, 67, 81–4; protects Siam, 68; and U.S. Civil War, 69; in World War II, 70–6, 79; postwar demands against Thailand, 80–1; and Malaya independence, 80, 85–6; and Singapore independence, 87–8, 90, 98; urges creation of Malaysia, 93, 97; relations with Indonesia, 101–2; Singapore leaves Malaysia, 109–10; and Sarawak, 114; development of Kuala Lumpur, 127, 129; *see also* British East India Company
Guerrilla activity: World War II,

Guerrilla activity (*cont.*)
77–9; postwar, 84, 86; in
Borneo, 97, 99, 102–3, 109, 111;
in Johore, 100–1; Communist,
138
Gullick, J. M., 138
Gunong Tahan (mountain), 3
Gutta-percha, 51

Hainan, 70
Hai San Society, 56
Hakka, Chinese, 143
Hang Tuah, 11
Hastings, Lord, 28
Himalaya Mountains, 2
Hindu culture in Southeast Asia,
31, 133, 134
Hindus in Malaya, 6, 7, 11, 115
Hitam, Musa, 126
Hiu Siew, 129
Holidays in Singapore, 51–2
Houses, 29, 42, 47, 63, 121, *131*,
132; Borneo long houses, 44;
in Petaling Jaya, 129; developments, 137
Hull, Cordell, 72
Hussein, Sultan, 26–7

Ice Age, 4
Independence: movement in Malaya, 80–5; Merdeka, 85–6;
movement in Singapore, 87–91,
93; independence declared, 98
Independence of Malaya Party,
84
India, 1, 4, 19, 29, 32, 53, 71;
trade, 2, 5, 7, 10, 16, 36; Portuguese take Goa, 14; independence, 83; *see also* British East
India Company
Indians: in Malaya, 68–9, 77, 81,
82, 85, 105; in Singapore, 112;
in Malaysia, 115, 116, 120, 121,
123, 125, 127
Indochina: French in, 59, 67–8,
83; Japan takes in World
War II, 70–2
Indonesia, 2, 5, 28, 38, 65, 69, 76,
83, 110; opposition to Malaysia
nation, ix, x, 91, 93–9, 108;
proposed union with Malaya,
81; invasions into Malaysia,
100–3; and United Nations,
103, 112; guerrillas in Borneo,
109, 111; anti-Communist insurrection, 111–12
Industry, 48–51, 68, 105, 113,
127; in Petaling Jaya, 129; in
Singapore, 139; *see also* Rubber industry; Tin industry
Ipoh, 133
Iron mines, 68
Islam, 8, 10, 11, 50, 52, 64, 94,
103, 130; marriage, 133–4
Italy, 70

Japan, 16; war with China, 70,
72, 74, 76; in World War II,
70–6; attacks Singapore, 73–6;
occupation of Malaya, 76–80
Java, 1, 2, 7, 11, 20, 76, 98; Raffles
in, 21–2, 31, 35; in thirteenth
century, 32
Java Man, 4
Jervois, Sir W. F. D., 58–61
Jesselton, 77–8
Johnson, Charles: *see* Brooke,
Charles
Johore Bahru, 15
Johore state, 5, 37, 52, 60, 68, 80,
81; wars with Malacca, 14, 15;
and Raffles, 26, 28; in World
War II, 74, 75; Indonesian
guerrilla invasion, 100–1

Index

Kalimantan, 94–5, 97, 100, 101, 111
Kampong, *131*, 133
Kedah, Sultan of, 68
Kedah state, 7, 18, 19, 37, 61, 77, 81, 138
Kelantan state, 37, 61, 68, 73, 77, 98
Kennedy, John F., 100
Kennedy, Robert, 100
Keppel, Captain Henry, 47
Khmers of Cambodia, 7
Kia Ba Ba, 141
Kipling, Rudyard, xi
Klang River, 127–9
Kuala Lumpur, 106, 108, 113, *124*, *130*, 136, 139, *142;* capital of Malaysia, 99, 107, 125; racial riots, 116–20; present-day, 127; founding, 128–9
Kuantan, 73–4
Kuching, 43, 46, 47, 53

Labor unions, 80
Land Dayaks, 41
Land erosion, 2–3
Langkasuka (legendary state), 7
Language, 105, 120–1
Laos, 67–8
Lee Kuan Yew, 15; forms government in Singapore, 87–9; advocates union with Malaysia, 88–91; declares Singapore's independence, 98; 1964 elections, 104–5; organizes Malaysia Solidarity Convention, 106–7; meets with Tunku, 108; after Singapore's expulsion from Malaysia, 108–11, 113; anti-American, 110; riots in Singapore, 120; present-day Singapore, 139, 141, 143

Legends: sky demons, 3; Badang, 32; spirits, 61; ancestors and creation, 62; world end, 63
Lela, Rajah, 60
Light, Captain Francis, 18–19
Lim Joo Suan, 141
Lim Yew-hock, 87
Long house, 44
Louis XVIII, King of France, 20
Low, Sir Hugh, 61, 64, 65
Lubuan Island, 47, 53–4, 61
Lundu River, 43

Macapagal, President of Philippines, 95–6
MacArthur, General Douglas, 78
Macintosh, Charles, 65
Madjapahit, 7, 8
Magellan, Ferdinand, 42
Mahmud Shah, 13, 14
Makota, 43, 45–6
Malacca, 80, 81, 133; founding, 8–10; Sultanate, 10–13; Portuguese in, 13–16; captured by Dutch, 16, 88; British in, 18, 20, 36–8, 49
Malay advisory councils, 78
Malay Annals, 11–13
Malay Nationalist Party, 81
Malay Peninsula, 16, 37, 55; geography, 1–3; settlement, 4–5, 7, 49
Malay rights, 105, 107, 113
Malay Union proposed, 81–2
Malaya, Federation of: formation, 67; settlements decline to join, 68; Union to Federation, 81–4; independence, 85–6; proposal for Singapore to join, 88–91; becomes Malaysia, 99
Malaya, Unfederated States of, 68, 77, 81

Malaya University, 121
Malayan Chinese Association (MCA), 85, 104, 106, 115, 117, 118, 127
Malayan Communist Party, 78–81, 88, 90, 138
Malayan Democratic Union, 81
Malayan Indian Congress, 85, 104, 116
Malayan People's Anti-Japanese Army (MPAJA), 79, 83, 107
Malays: fear of Chinese, x–xi, 49, 98, 105–7, 119, 138; physical characteristics, 5
Malaysia: formation, ix, x, 97, 99; formation proposed, 90–8; objections by Indonesia, 91, 93–8; Philippine claims to territory, 91, 95; today, 125, 137–9, 141, 143
Malaysia Solidarity Convention, 106–7, 110, 111
Mao Tse-tung, 81
Maphilindo, 96
Marriage in Malaysia, 64, 115, 133–4
Marsden, William, 21, 22, 24
Marshall, David, 86–7
Martaban (ship), 69
Melanesians, 5
Merdeka: see Independence
Midway, Battle of, 78
Miller, Harry, 41, 61, 88
Mineral resources: see Tin industry
Ming dynasty, 8
Minto, Lord, 21
Moluccas: see Spice Islands
Mongkut, King of Siam, 68
Monsoons, 2–3
Mountains, 2–3
Muda Japhar, Rajah, 26

Mudah, Rajah, 43–6
Muddy River Mouth, 129
Muslims: see Islam
Mutahir, Tun, 13–15
Myths: see Legends

Nagumo, Admiral Chuichi, 73
Nair, Devan, 113
Nakhoda Ragam, 42
Naning state, 38
Napoleon, 20, 22
Nasution, General, 112
National Mosque, *130*
National Operations Council, 118, 123
National Parliament Building, *142*
Negri Sembilan, 37, 60, 67, 81, 133
Negritos, 5
Netherlands: in Malaya, 15, 88; war with Spain, 15–16; relations with Great Britain, 19, 20, 22–4, 28, 35–7, 59; held island of Rhio, 26; cedes Malacca to Great Britain, 36–7; expansion, 38; settlement in Brunei, 43; in Borneo, 55, 71; lost Indonesia, 83
New Guinea, 78
New Nation (Singapore), 141
Newsweek, 118
Ningkan, Dato, 114
Nippon Times (Tokyo), 72
Nomura, Kichisaburo, 72
North Borneo (Sabah), x, 1, 3, 5, 43, 47; administered by Dent, 54–5; in World War II, 77–8; proposed as part of Malaysia, 90, 92–8; Philippine claim on, 95–6; guerrilla warfare, 97, 99, 109; became Sabah, 98; after

Index

Singapore leaves Malaysia, 109, 111, 112; elections suspended, 118

Oil in Brunei, 77, 93, 96
Omar Ali, Sultan, 43, 45–7, 49
Onn bin Ja'afar, Dato, 82, 84
Opium War, 19–20
Ord, Governor, 55

Pahang state, 12, 37, 67, 81
Palembang, Dutch station at, 22
Paleolithic culture, 4–5
Palm oil, 66, 113
Pan-Malayan Islamic Party of Kelantan, 98
Pandak Indut, 60
Pangkor Island, 56
Paramesvara, founds Malacca, 7–10, 23
Pasir Salik, 60
Pearl Harbor, 71–4
Pearl River, 70
Peking Man, 4
Penang Island, 80, 81; British port, 18–21, 28, 36–8, 49, 105; Georgetown, 133
People's Action Party (PAP), 87–9, 104, 114
Perak, Tun, 11–13, 15, 16
Perak state, 81, 133; River Valley, 4; ruled by Malaccan sultans, 37; tin mining, 49, 56, 129; British Residents in, 56–61, 67; Communist penetration, 138
Percival, A. E., 75–6
Perlis state, 68, 77, 81
Petaling Jaya, 129
Philip II of Spain, 15, 16
Philippine Islands, 1, 5, 41, 45, 94; claim on North Borneo, ix–x, 95–6; sacked by Bulkiah, 42; in World War II, 73, 77, 78; opposition to Malaysia nation, 91, 93, 95–7; relations with Malaysia broken, 99; relations restored, 113
Phoenicians, 1, 5
Pickering, W. A., 56
Pigafetta, Antonio, 42
Pirates, 26, 27, 52, 55, 56, 64; Dayaks, 41–2; suppressed by Brooke, 47
Political developments: in Malaya, 81–5; in Singapore, 86–8; *see also* Malayan Communist Party; People's Action Party; United Malays National Organization
Polygamy, 64
Port Swettenham, 57, 139
Portugal, 13–16, 88
Press, 118
Priestly, Joseph, 65
Prince of Wales (ship), 71–4
Proclamation of Laws, Raffles, 33–4
Puteh, Tun, 13

Racism in Malaysia: against Chinese, x–xi, 49, 90, 105–6, 112–14, 121, 138–9; segregation, 115, 121; riots, 116–20, 138; employment, 126
Radio and television, 136
Raffles, Thomas Stamford, 39, 50, 59, 140; background, 21; governor of Bencoolen, 22; founds Singapore, 22–4, 26; statue, 25; treaty with Hussein, 26–7, 36; quarrels with Farquhar, 27, 29, 30, 32–3; policies in Singapore, 28–31; Proclama-

Raffles, Thomas Stamford (cont.)
  tion of Laws, 33-4; shipwreck and death, 35
Railroads, 64
Rainfall, 3
Rakyat Party, 94
Razak, Tun: see Abdul Razak, Tun
Religion, 49-50, 94; marriage, 115, 133-4; see also Buddhism; Catholicism; Hindus; Islam
Repulse (ship), 71-4
Residents system, 56-61, 67, 82
Rhio Island, 24, 26
Riau Sultanate, 37
Rice harvest dance, 134
Riots, 103, 116-20, 123
River-states in Malaya, 49
Robespierre, 20
Romans, 1, 5, 15
Roosevelt, Franklin D., 71
Rubber industry, 65-7, 77, 78, 137
"Running amok," 119
Russia, 20, 78, 79, 102, 103, 109, 110

Sabah: see North Borneo (Sabah)
St. Helena, 22
Sang Nila Utama, 23, 24
Sarawak, 1, 3, *41*, 77; Dayak rebellion, 43-5; proposed as part of Malaysia, 90, 92, 94, 96-8; after Singapore leaves Malaysia, 109, 111, 112; 1966 crisis, 114; elections suspended, 118; Communism in, 138; White Rajahs: see Brooke, Charles; Brooke, James
Sea Dayaks, 41-2
Secret societies, Chinese, 50, 52, 53, 55-6, 78, 105, 129

Semmes, Captain, 69
Sengalor state, 57, 81; tin mining, 49; piracy, 56; Sweetenham in, 61, 64; in proposed Federation, 67; Kuala Lumpur as capital, 117, 118
Seremban, 133
Shadow plays (Wayang Kulit), 134
Shell Oil Company, 94
Siam, 37, 59, 61; controls Tumasik, 8; threat to Malacca, 10-11; threat to Kedah, 19; British protection, 68; see also Thailand
Silat Buah, 134
Singapore, x, 67; founding by Raffles, 7, 19, 21-4, 26-8, 33; ancient history, 23-4; expansion of trade, 28-9, 36-8, 48, 49, 51, 69, 108-11, 139; nineteenth century life in, 30-1; stones and legends, 31-2; tigers in, 52; crime, 52-3; *Alabama* affair, 69; in World War II, 70-7, 79; postwar, 81, 82; Communists in, 86-8; proposals to join Malaysia, 88-93, 97; independence, 98; riots in, 103, 120; expelled from Malaysia, 108-11; after expulsion, 109-13; current conditions in, 139, 141, 143
Singapore River, *140*
Singapura: see Singapore
Singora, 73
Siniawan Dayaks, 46
Sky demons, legend of, 3
Slavery, 58, 60
Slimming, John, 106, 117, 121
Socialism in Singapore, 88, 89, 106, 110

Index

South China Sea, 1, 3, 8
Spain, 15–16, 95–6
Speedy, Captain, 57
Spice Islands (Moluccas), 1, 2, 10, 11, 20, 22
Spice trade, 10, 15, 16, 50
Sports, 51–2
Sri, son of Paramesvara, 10–11
Sri Vijaya, 7
Stephens, Dato, 109
Stone Age, 4–5
Straits of Malacca, 1, 8, 56, 132
Straits Settlements, 37, 48, 55–6, 58, 67, 68, 81, 93
Straits of Singapore, 26, 52, 75
Straits Times (Singapore), 32, 61, 63, 69, 88
Strikes, 78
Suharto, General, 112
Sukarno, President of Indonesia, ix, 94–100, 103, 111–12
Sulu, Sultan of, 54, 95
Sulu Sea, 42
Sumatra, 1, 2, 11, 21, 35, 36, 136
Sunda Platform 2, 41
Sunda Straits, 69
Sungei Ujong, 60
Swettenham, Sir Frank, 56; Assistant Resident, 57; escapes assassination, 60; in Sengalor state, 61, 64; *Malay Sketches*, 63; Federation plan, 67; High Commissioner of Straits Settlements, 68; Union proposal, 82; Kuala Lumpur rebuilding, 129

Tan Siew Sin, 115, 117, 118, 127
Tea trade, 17
Thailand, 1, 4, 5, 80–1, 86, 138; in World War II, 71–3, 76–7; *see also* Siam
Tigers, 52

Time, 118
Times (London), 95, 118
Tin industry, 49–50, 56, 68, 77, 78, 105, 129, 137
Tjondonegro, Suwardjo, 101
Trade, 1–2, 125; Malay settlements, 5, 7, 20–1; spices, 10, 16; Malacca, 11, 15; Great Britain, 17–24; Singapore, 22–4, 26–9, 36–8, 48, 49, 51, 69, 108–11, 139; decline during World War II, 77; and threat of Socialism, 88
Tregonning, K. C., 23, 27, 28
Trengganu state, 61, 68, 77, 81
Tumasik, 7, 8, 23
Tunku, the: *see* Abdul Rahman (the Tunku)

U Thant, 97–9
Unfederated States of Malaya, 68, 77, 81
United Malays National Organization (UMNO), 82, 84–5, 104, 106, 116–17
United Nations: Commission on creation of Malaysia, 96–9; Malaysia joins, 100; complaint to Security Council, 101–2; Malaysia seat on Council, 103–4; Indonesia leaves and returns, 103, 112
United States, 19, 55, 70, 96, 115, 123, 126; racism, x, xi; cotton exports, 69; Civil War, 69; in World War II, 71–4, 77, 79, 80; Robert Kennedy visits Indonesia, 100; Lee's anti-U.S. campaign, 110

Vietnam, 2, 5, 7, 67, 72, 100, 110, 138

Villages, 42, 63, *132; Kampong,*
  131, 133
Von Overbeck, Baron, 54, 95
Vyner Brooke (ship), 76

Wavell, General Archibald, 75–6
West Malaysia, 1, 3, 109, 114
White Rajah: *see* Brooke, James
Wilson, Harold, 110

Women, 64
World War II, 70–80; postwar, 80–3

Yamashita, Tomoyuki, 76
Yang di-Pertuan Agong (Supreme Ruler), 85–6, 93
Youth, 121–2, 134
Yusuf, Rajah, 60

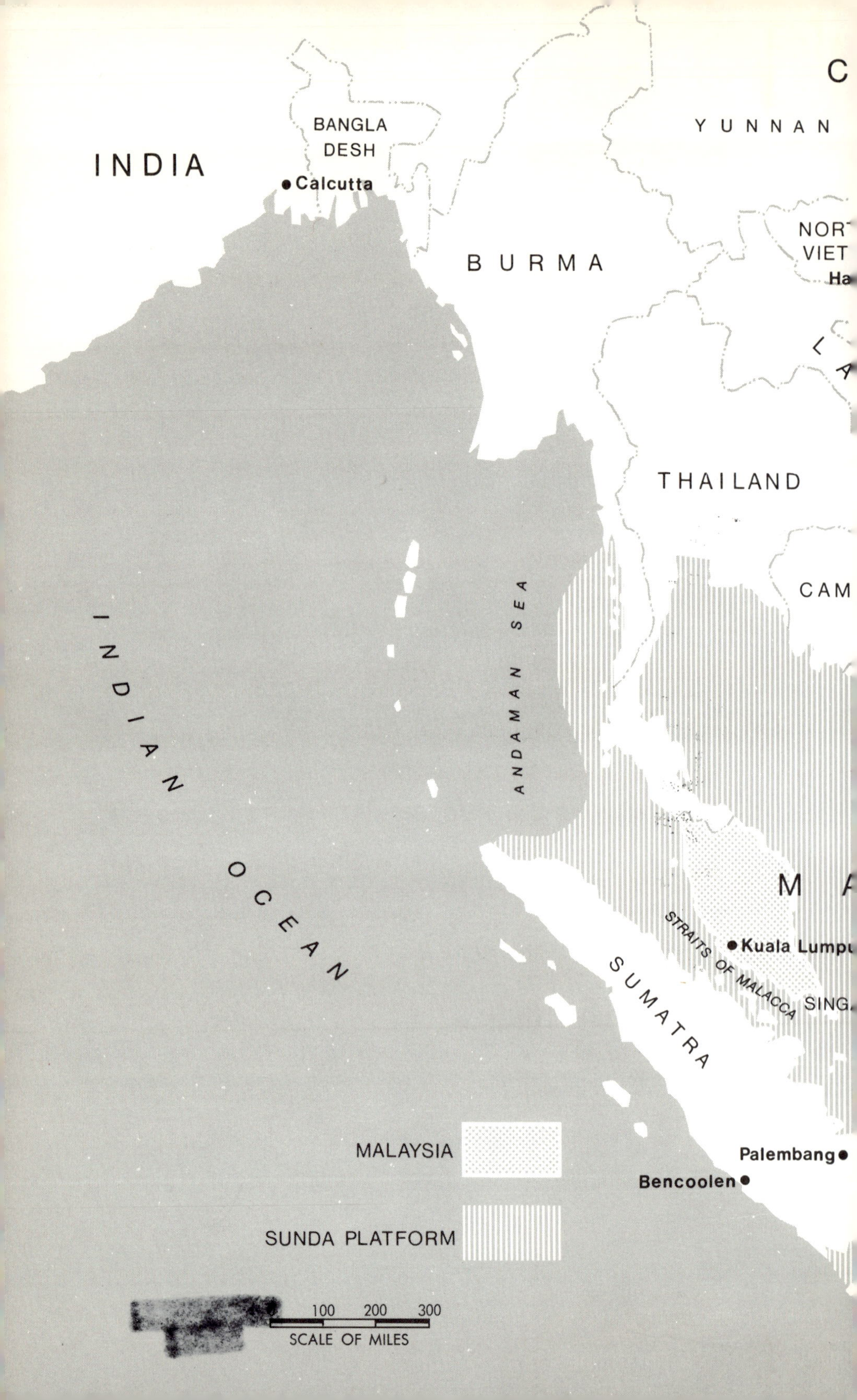
BANGLA
DESH
INDIA
Calcutta
YUNNAN
BURMA
THAILAND
ANDAMAN SEA
INDIAN OCEAN
STRAITS OF MALACCA
SUMATRA
Palembang
Bencoolen
MALAYSIA
SUNDA PLATFORM
100
200
300
SCALE OF MILES